THE ART OF JAPANESE GARDENING

1 *Kiyoshi Saito:* Snow in the evening sunlight

2 A stone water basin with bamboo pipe

3 Garden lantern among clipped bushes

4 *Metal lanterns and wisteria. Wisteria is particularly popular in large temple gardens and for* kaiyu *gardens*

THE ART OF
JAPANESE GARDENING

Text by Zdeněk Hrdlička
and Věnceslava Hrdličková
Photographs by Zdeněk Thoma
Edited by Takashi Sawano

HAMLYN

Designed and produced by Artia
for The Hamlyn Publishing Group Limited,
a division of The Octopus Publishing Group,
Michelin House, 81 Fulham Road,
London SW3 6RB, England

Text by Zdeněk Hrdlička and Věnceslava Hrdličková
Translated by Iris Urwin
Edited by Takashi Sawano
Photographs by Zdeněk Thoma
Graphic design by Aleš Krejča

ISBN 0 600 55110 5
Printed in Czechoslovakia by Tisk, n. p., knižní výroba, závod 6, Brno
2/99/70/51-01

PHOTOGRAPHIC CREDITS

Zdeněk Hrdlička and Věnceslava Hrdličková: 12, 14, 15, 23, 50, 54, 56, 62, 65, 69, 72, 79–81, 91, 93, 99, 107, 109, 113, 115, 117, 123, 124, 130, 135, 138, 141, 144, 160, 161, 163, 172, 178, 183, 186, 191, 202, 207, 209, 212–214, 218, 220, 226, 229, 232, 235, 237, 240, 244, 251, 259, 261, 263, 270, 280
Václav Kašpar: 188
Otakar Kuča: 154
Zdeněk Thoma: 1–11, 13, 16–22, 24–49, 51–53, 55, 57–61, 66–68, 70, 71, 73–78, 82–90, 92, 94–98, 100–106, 108, 110–112, 114, 116, 118–122, 125–129, 131–134, 136, 137, 139, 140, 142, 143, 145–153, 155–159, 162, 164–171, 173–177, 179–182, 184, 185, 187, 189, 190, 192–201, 203–205, 208, 210, 211, 215–217, 219, 221–225, 227, 228, 230, 231, 233, 234, 236, 238, 239, 241–243, 245–250, 252–258, 260, 262, 264–269, 271–279, 281–284
Ivan Tichý: 206

◀ 5 *A ceramic dish from Kutani decorated with a painting of a garden landscape*

6 *A water basin with scoops and a metal dragon, Kiyomizu, Kyoto*

Contents

Introduction

The Japanese have always considered nature to be the essence of beauty, and have endeavoured to integrate this philosophy into their everyday lives. Even such simple things as drinking tea, taking a meal, or arranging flowers have acquired an aesthetic dimension, and over the centuries the Japanese brought to perfection a conception of refined elegance which is the key to understanding all Japanese forms of artistic expression.

Gardens are an art form and the

7 *Boats on a garden lake, Heian period. Painted on a fan, by an unknown artist, 17th century*

8 *The island of Sado, part of the coast*

creators of the traditional Japanese gardens are compared to poets; the only difference being that instead of words gardens used the elements of nature itself — stones, moss, water and trees — to express their ideas. It was their aim to bring to mankind the very essence of natural scenery, in however small a space, and thus to create an atmosphere in which the soul can be at rest after the distractions of the daily round.

If we are to understand Japanese gardens we must be patient, for they are imbued with so many purely Japanese qualities that they cannot readily be appreciated in all their variety without due regard for the broader cultural context within which they are set.

9 Mountain scenery; the Komagatake volcano in eruption

10 Fallen trees by a lake

Japanese gardens are the work of men's hands and of intellectual genius. They are no mere imitation of nature but a living portrayal of their creators' vision of nature. They bear all the hallmarks of a work of art.

The perfect view of nature expressed in Japanese gardens was not attained either quickly or easily. It is the work of generations of educated artists and simple gardeners, from the earliest times when spacious gardens were the scene of aristocratic entertainment, through the Middle Ages when Zen philosophy exercised a remarkable influence on garden design, to the dry garden and the tea garden, right through to the parks and the residential gardens of today.

Over these centuries the Japanese developed a highly specific code of beauty in which simplicity, the art of suggestion and restraint in emotions and colours are particularly characteristic. It also includes a preference for objects marked by asymmetry, by the patina of age, and by nostalgia and melancholy — which always touches any human being.

All this has left its mark on the conception of any garden design, whose ultimate aim, as the 16th-century aesthete Soami said, was 'to portray by means of the simplest things the mystery of nature and its creation'.

This means that if we learn how to treat stones, water and plants in an artistic way, we shall be able to recognize the infinite ocean in a tiny garden pond, while a moss-covered stone will breathe the majesty of a great mountain upon us.

It is a simple concept, and yet it is

12 *Sesshu:* Landscape, *early 16th century*

11 *Akisato Rito:* Sakureizu, *title page of a gardeners' handbook, 18th century*

13 A stone lantern, Nikko

15 A stone lantern by a path (woodcut)

14 A stone lantern in the rankei *style overhanging the water (woodcut)*

an infinitely difficult one to grasp. It calls for 'a pure soul', as the Japanese say, for great self-discipline, and for ability to adhere consistently to the laws of the art of garden design while at the same time having the creative courage to go beyond them.

Garden design conformed to a firm set of guidelines right from the outset. A code was handed down by word of mouth, and also written down in the secret handbooks used by members of the gardeners' guild. Today these handbooks are still an invaluable source of information on the traditional art of the Japanese garden.

The art of the Japanese gardeners was always akin to painting, particularly to ink drawings in which a few masterly lines portray the essential features of a bamboo stem, a flowering plum branch, or mountain scenery. From such paintings the gardeners learnt the rules of spatial composition, and how to make use of light and shade; from paintings, too, they learnt the art of giving an inner rhythm to their design.

The Japanese gardener is dealing with a clearly defined space, marked off by a fence or wall, just as the painter has before him a scroll of white paper or silk. And just as the painters spent years practising each of the individual components of their pictures — from simple lines to the stem of bamboo or the contours of a mountain — until they could catch the essential likeness — so the gardeners needed their years of apprenticeship. It took a long time before they would venture to create on their own. They proceeded slowly, step by step. They learned to understand the harmony of the forces of nature, to form ponds and streams, to plant trees and shrubs, to recognize the shapes of stones and position them in the garden, and to combine all these

16 *A garden bridge leading to an island in the Nijo garden, Kyoto*

elements in a symbolic composition so that the garden expressed a certain idea. Most often that idea was of longevity, of human happiness, and the relationship of man to nature.

The Japanese make use of qualities which craftsmen and artists in other parts of the world rarely take into consideration. For example, the nature of the raw materials used; they see beauty in the rough, the irregular, even in the commonplace. Colours are not sought for their richness, but for their shades and the harmony of their tones. In choosing shapes, it is not perfection which is sought, but the irregular in all its variety, for this bears witness to the changes, the contingencies, the adversities that everything in nature is subject to; and that human beings cannot avoid, either. It is seen in a glint of sunlight

17 *Composition: a clipped tree with a garden lantern*

on the waters of a lake, fallen leaves twisting in the current of a stream; it is heard in the breeze. Man is not alone the creator of gardens; nature is ever-present, bringing about those changes which the human hand cannot give. Nature refreshes the garden with rain and covers it with a blanket of snow in winter; the sun's rays warm it, and enrich or subdue its colours.

What pleasure all this can give to those who are perceptive! In Japan a sensitive awareness of nature became the very basis of life and art. To achieve their goal the gardeners

18 A cypress tree painted on a 16th-century fan

used signs and symbols to express the essential inward and outward features of nature. These artists of the garden chose the most exact and the most restrained means of expression, demonstrating the links between the art of the garden and that of the *haiku*[2)], the poems in which a few simple words sufficed to express a profound thought. In this way Japanese gardeners achieved in a restricted space an image of nature in all her grandeur.

Once the basic methods had been defined, it was possible to reduce the size of the gardens further and further, without impairing their imagery, as can be seen in the miniature gardens created within the space of a single bowl.

The principles and techniques of Japanese garden design, its refinement of composition, the bold use of such materials as stones and sand, and above all the integration of the garden into the house, are all featured in modern architectural design. Although their importance was discovered long ago in Japan, for a very different way of life, these principles seem made for life today.

The traditional gardens of Japan are primarily the expression of the dynamic integration of space with content, and have the most intimate bonds with man. With the experience of centuries behind them, they pass into a sphere free from conventional thought. They point the way to inner peace and repose. It is this aspect that brings so traditional an art as that of the Japanese garden astonishingly close to the needs of man in the modern world.

19 *Traditional garden features complement high-rise buildings, Shinjuku, Tokyo*

20 *Kiyoshi Saito:* Stone garden, Kyoto ▸

Kiyoshi Saito

21 A gravel garden at the Shinto shrine in Isa

They sat together in silence,
the host, the guest and
the white chrysanthemum.
Ryota

The origins of Japanese gardens

The roots of Japanese gardening go far back into the past, when the great diversity of natural beauty found in this country of islands, which has always inspired the people both emotionally and creatively, gave rise to Shinto, their earliest religion.

Then, in the 6th century, a new religion found its way to Japan through the corridor of Korea. Unlike Shinto, this religion was splendid in its ceremony and profound in its spirituality, and it caught the imagination of simple people and artists alike. It was Buddhism, although not the original form of the religion, but one tempered by Chinese thought. It was a form influenced strongly by the Taoist pursuit of harmony between man and nature in the natural course of events. This was a fortunate combination, for the native Shinto religion with its very simple worship of the forces of nature was directed to the same goal. Thus it did not clash with Buddhism, but each form of worship influenced and interwove with the other, although Shinto maintained its

22 A shinden *style house and garden of the Heian period. Detail of a painting on a fan; probably 12th century*

independent existence and remained an integral part of Japanese thought for many centuries.

Along with Buddhism the land of Yamato, as Japan was then called, also received a highly developed civilization from China which included their script. Having as yet no written language of their own, the Japanese took over the intricate yet undoubtedly attractive system of characters used by the Chinese, and became acquainted with Chinese thought and political organization, whose traditions, even in the 6th century, went far back into the past.

It is amazing how resourcefully the Japanese dealt with this incoming flood of culture and information,

23 *A plan of a garden in the* shinden-zukuri *style, Tosanjo*

24 *The Imperial Palace, Kyoto, reconstructed in 1855. In front of the entrance there is a sand garden with two trees, one of which is visible in this photograph*

adapting it and giving it their own character to create one of the most remarkable civilizations in the world. The artistic and philosophical expression of the Japanese created new dimensions of beauty, many of which are singularly appropriate to the mind of modern man.

This first period from the middle of the 6th century when knowledge of

China came to Japan largely through Korea, up to the year 724 when Japan established direct relations with the great and powerful T'ang empire[3], was marked by assiduous efforts to assimilate all that was new. The political structure of Japan was to be changed overnight by a series of measures and reforms, and no expense was spared to deck out the court of Japan in all the magnificence displayed by its mighty neighbour on the mainland.

In this spirit it was decided to build a Japanese capital similar to Ch'ang-an in China. This was a revolutionary decision when one remembers the Japanese custom of deserting the imperial palace, which was a fairly simple timber-built structure, the

25 *The principal building of the Imperial Palace in Kyoto, the Shishinden, with the audience chamber. The area in front of the building is covered with a deep layer of white sand, with a lemon tree on the left and a flowering cherry on the right, and recalls the first gardens of the* shinden *palaces of the Heian period*

moment it was marked by the death of the monarch, in order to set up a new one, even if it was usually not very far away.

At the beginning of the 8th century, in what is known as the Nara period[4], a capital city was established in central Japan, apparently with the help of craftsmen from China and Korea. Called Heijokyo[5], it remained the seat of seven successive emperors. The next step, following two rapid moves which have still not been satisfactorily explained, was the building of a permanent imperial city; called Heiankyo (City of Peace and Concord) it was the centre of Japanese life for almost three centuries, during the Heian period[6], and later under the name of Kyoto was the seat of the emperors of Japan up to the middle of the 19th century.

As architecture developed during the Nara and Heian periods, so the art of the Japanese gardens came into being, an art which was always the expression of a cultivated life-style. The Heian gardens evolved under the influence not only of the Chinese, but of the Japanese attitude to nature, for which Shinto was still seminal.

In the distant past the people of the Japanese islands believed that a mysterious and inexplicable force pervaded the whole of the material world and all space. The primary symbol of this force was stone. Gradually, as the pantheon of the Shinto gods was formed, sacred places where rites were performed were set aside. They were carefully delimited, and strewn with sand and pebbles. The Japanese sense of the beauty in nature and their treatment of space was strength-

26 *The Mino palace, Kyoto*

27 *The outer garden of the Imperial Palace, with the Mino palace in the background*

ened, and became apparent in the art of the garden.

The custom of surrounding the tombs of deceased rulers with a landscape undoubtedly contributed to the development of garden design[7]; these tombs, which lay on islands in artificial lakes, were planted with trees (as far as can be judged from the surviving examples), while the shores of the lakes were strengthened and at the same time adorned with stones.

Gardens are more ephemeral than any other art form, and so even in Japan, where great care is taken of old-established gardens, and where the most beautiful have been declared national treasures, we have only fragmentary remains of the wealth of landscape gardens we know to have been created from the 7th to the end of the 12th centuries, for the city of Heiankyo was destroyed by fire at the beginning of the 13th century. The gardens of the time, fortunately, were so unforgettable and played such an important role in the social life of the time as the setting for aristocratic entertainment and amusement, that they found their way into poetry[8] and into the popular historical romances of the day. Painters and illustrators depicted them on their horizontal scrolls (*e-makimono*). The social life of the time is most clearly portrayed in 12th-century scroll paintings, particularly in the *Nenju gyoji e-maki* (Rites and ceremonies throughout the year).

Extremely valuable knowledge of Japanese gardens is to be found in two scroll manuscripts known as *Sakuteiki* (Notes on the making of gardens)[9]. These are usually attributed

28 *Usually only a single tree was planted in the ceremonial vicinity of the temple*

29 *Ceremonial water tank at the entrance to the Heian shrine, Kyoto*

to Yoshitsune Gokyogoku, who died in 1206. The very fact that such a work was written testifies to the importance of landscape gardening at that time.

The *Sakuteiki* scrolls were the first in the series of handbooks for gardeners. However, in the Middle Ages most of these books were secret, handed down from master to apprentice, from teacher to disciple, as was the custom in other Japanese guilds. The craftsmen were protecting themselves against those who would have liked to penetrate the secrets of their

30 *Stone lanterns at the Kasuga shrine, Nara*

skill and thus rob the members of the guild of their livelihood. Another reason is that the master believed that learning was gained from direct experience alone and not by the written word. The book describes only the master's experience and could be misconstrued by the apprentice. Good craftsmanship has always been highly regarded in Japan.

Landscape gardening enjoyed an age-long tradition in China and there were already several different styles developed by the 6th century. Indeed, the ruler of Japan received a stone for his garden among the gifts sent to him by the emperor of China. The works of the Chinese poet and lover of gardens, Po Chü-i, were very influential in Japan.

31 Metal lanterns in the Kasuga shrine, Nara

In Japan, as in China, the aesthetic rules for landscape gardening were largely influenced by the 'science' of the time, known in Europe under the not very exact name of geomancy, in China as *feng-shuei.* This was based on the Chinese view of nature and the world as the expression of harmony between the principle of *yang* (*yo* in Japanese), which represented light, virility and strength, and the principle of *yin* (Japanese *in*), which represented twilight, femininity, delicacy. Every disturbance of this harmony, every upset, brought down on man the malignity of the evil spirits which control nature in balance with the good spirits. It was therefore most important to avoid disturbing this harmony when building a house or planning a garden. This resulted in a complicated system of rules, prohibitions and injunctions. Although it was little more than a collection of superstitions, the method had its practical advantages. Both in China and Japan, *feng-shuei* influenced aesthetics so that both houses and gardens were designed as natural elements in the landscape. It was also desirable to achieve in the garden a harmonious balance between light and shade, curved and sharp contours, 'feminine delicacy' and 'masculine strength', according to the teaching of *in-yo*.

The symbolic significance of the numbers seven, five and three was also important, leading landscape gardeners to asymmetrical combinations of stones, bushes and trees. This principle is still accepted in the aesthetic principles of composition today.

Although the principles of *feng-shuei* seem very strict, even rigid, it was all to the good that they attempted to adapt the ideas of individual gardeners to the balance of nature, even when they had only a very small space at their command. According to the superstitions prevalent throughout eastern Asia, any deviation from these rules would mean the

32 *The beauty of the park surrounding the Itsukushima shrine is greatly enhanced by the movements of the tides which have been incorporated in the design. A* torii, *or wooden gateway, is a central feature of the scene*

possibility of evil consequences, even perhaps death.

Here, in fact, is the explanation of the need to design paths and garden walks which wind and twist, along which the forces of good and benevolence pass, while evil spirits choose only those paths which lead directly to their goal. It is no wonder that even today many Japanese feel their flesh creep at the sight of formal European gardens with their straight paths, while Europeans who try to make a Japanese garden without real knowledge of the ideas behind the art, are puzzled to see that they rarely achieve a satisfactory result.

Of the many types of the garden art practised in China it was the landscape gardens surrounding temples and palaces that first came to Japan[11]. During the Nara period these buildings seem at first to have been built in completely untouched surroundings separated from the rest of the countryside by a wall. This was certainly the case for the Nara capital, Heijokyo, where recent excavations have revealed the remains of a large park with a wall around it behind the mid-8th century palace of the emperor Shomu[12]. It was here that the Shorinkyu pine wood grew, which was mentioned in the *Shokunihongi* chronicle[13].

The new capital of Japan, Heian-kyo, was built on the pattern of the Chinese capital city, Ch'ang-an, in an area of beautiful mountains, hills and streams. Lying on a gentle slope, it was rectangular in plan and surrounded by a moat. Broad streets divided the town into square blocks which were further divided into smaller units by little streets. There were canals of running water along

33 *A metal lantern and* torii *at the Itsukushima shrine, Miyajima*

34 Fallow deer by the Itsukushima shrine, Miyajima. Deer were sacred animals and were often allowed to roam in temple gardens

each side of the main streets. The severity of the plan was softened by the movement of life in the city, which flourished yet always looked towards the north, where the rich and powerful lived in great mansions set in flower gardens, all centred round the seat of the emperor himself like bees in a swarm around their queen.

During the second half of the Heian period (from the end of the 9th century) the houses of the rich were designed in the *shinden-zukuri* style which, judging from contemporary scroll paintings, was a Japanese variant of the Chinese style. Like all the other ideas imported from China this was soon adapted by the Japanese to their own conditions and taste.

Both the imperial palace and the mansions of the rich were built in this style, with the difference that the emperor's palace was larger and the part set aside for ritual use was of greater importance. This can be seen fairly clearly from the imperial palace of Kyoto, restored in 1855.

Shinden architecture was well suited to the warm climate in this central region of Japan, and also to the lively social life at the imperial court and in the houses of the rich. Some of the designs then in fashion are followed today. A palace in *shinden* style covered a considerable area; the principal building, known as *shinden* (literally 'the palace for sleep'), was linked with a pavilion to the west and with covered galleries to the east.

The light and airy wooden buildings were integrated with a landscape garden on the south side of the central building, designed at great expense to give the impression of a natural landscape. One of the garden's main attractions was the free use of water, of which there was no shortage in and around Heian. Water was as essential a component of the garden as were the artificial mounds and hillocks. At a certain distance from the *shinden* the garden contained a lake with an island in it, and from this feature the whole garden was at first referred to as an 'island' (*shima*).

At the point nearest to the house the island was connected to the rest of the garden by an arched bridge while a level bridge served the same purpose on the south side. A fishing pavilion usually stood on that side together with a spring of water protected by a roof. A little brook ran into the lake from the east, and out again on the western side.

Little paths wound through the garden, among bushes, trees and coloured patches of flowers that provided a constant change in the scenery season by season. Contemporary scroll paintings suggest that coniferous trees joined company with cherry, maple, and plum trees. Following the Chinese custom, it had become fashionable to plant flowering plums, yet these hardy little trees, blossoming before the onset of Spring with no fear of the snowstorms to come, never quite overcame the admiration the Japanese had for the flowering cherry. The supple stems and delicate leaves of the bamboo lent an air of elegance to these gardens and favourite flowers were azaleas, irises, peonies, lilies and chrysanthemums. As a rule a twisted pine tree grew on the island. There was a symbolical significance attached to both trees and flowers, related to the ideas of longevity, everlasting happiness and of being blessed.

Level ground was enlivened by artificial mounds, stones and waterfalls, and all the elements were arranged so as to form a harmonious whole. The principles of light and shade, strength and delicacy, masculinity and femininity were kept in balance, and it was firmly believed that insensitive disturbance of natural harmony could have disastrous consequences.

No wonder that the *Sakuteiki* impressed upon its readers that 'when making a garden it is essential to observe the natural shapes of the lakes, and to form hills and streams that conform to natural outlines . . . The first task, therefore, is to dig the lake in harmony with the surrounding landscape, and only then to pile up an artificial hill and lay a path in accordance with the shape of the lake.'

We can form some idea of what the palaces and gardens of the Heian period looked like, from the reconstruction of the plan of the Tosanjo palace[14], which belonged to the Fujiwara family, one of the most powerful families in Japan. In addition to the usual buildings the plan shows a pavilion for musicians where they would have played for the company boating on the lake. There were three islands in the lake in the Tosanjo garden: the first island was linked to the mainland by an arched bridge, the second was reached by a level bridge, and access to the third was over a drawbridge which could be raised for boats to pass under (see page 20). To the south-east of the western corridor was a garden of wild flowers

35 Traditional post top used on garden bridges and railings.

36 *The Kofukuji pagoda, Nara, with tall pine trees. This pagoda was first erected in 730* AD

and grasses. During the Heian period gardens were designed by well-known poets and painters, of whom the most famous were Kudara no Kawanari, Kose no Kanaoka and Kose no Hirotaka.

Although gardens were the work of men their effect was unforced and natural, for careful thought had gone into their design, and their creators had worked in harmony with nature. This accounts for the great variety seen in all the component parts. Waterfalls might be straight, angled, powerful, tiny, split into two; lakes varied greatly in shape according to the type of landscape the garden was intended to represent. Islands bore a symbolic significance, and in the Heian period this often related to the old Taoist legend of the islands of the immortals in the Eastern Sea. One of the islands was Horai (in Chinese, P'eng Lai-shan), where the elixir of life gushed from a jadeite cliff. The legend tells how the emperor of China, Ch'in Shih-huang, sent a company of beautiful youths and maidens to find the island and bring him the elixir, in the year 219 BC. According to one version of the legend they were already in sight of the islands when an unfavourable wind arose and prevented them from landing.

In Japanese gardens the island of Horai was the symbol of longevity, and so it was often given the shape of a tortoise or crane; symbols of long life — the tortoise was supposed to be able to live for ten thousand years, and the crane for a thousand. The boats which sailed to the island, in the legend, were represented in the garden by stones grouped between the island and the shore of the lake; these were called *yodomariishi* ('stones of waiting by night'). In different forms, these symbols of the island of Horai remained a constant feature of Japanese gardens.

Long life, happiness and beatitude

37 *Lacquer bowl decorated with a pagoda in a garden*

were also symbolized by the animals the owners kept in these Heian gardens; for instance, the goldfish in the ponds, and the mandarin ducks and the snow white cranes on the shores of the lakes.

It is clear from the sources at our disposal that it was fashionable in the Heian period to design gardens based on famous beauty-spots, like Ama-no-Hashidate [15] (the Bridge of the Gods), which is still one of the most beautiful places in Japan.

The artists of the time went to remarkable efforts to make their gardens an expression of reality. We learn from old records that the nobleman Minamoto Toru had islands planted with pines made in the lakes of his garden so as to form a replica of the lovely Bay of Shiogama. To complete the illusion, during his garden parties he even had fires lit on the shores of the lake, just as the fishermen did when they burned seaweed to collect salt on the shores of the Bay.

Another nobleman ordered pure

38 *The five-storied Yukushiji pagoda, Nara*

39 *Kiyomizu temple and garden, decoration on a kimono*

40 *View of the Okuno-in pavilion where forest trees form part of the landscape garden, Kiyomizudera*

white sea salt to be heaped along the edge of his garden lake to create the most realistic impression of the seashore.

The climate of Japan, particularly round Kyoto – then Heian – was temperate, so that the aristocracy could spend time in their gardens most of the year round. The life of these nobles and the life of the garden became interdependent, and many superstitions arose from this intimacy, with direct consequences for garden design. It was believed that a flat stone placed in the 'sleeping position' near the bedroom of the master of the house would bring about his premature death; if a garden stone was placed parallel to a pillar of the house, misfortune would befall the descendants. There was another superstition that a valley cut out of an artificial hill and leading straight towards the house would have evil consequences for the owner's daughter. All this led the garden designers to avoid symmetry, which never looks natural anyway. The warning against planting a single tree in the centre of the garden is still observed as it recalls the Chinese character for *komaru* – to land in trouble.

This blend of practical advice, experience of life, fear of adversity, of longing for happiness, together with the Japanese natural affinity for nature, produced a code of aesthetics which has a great deal of symbolic significance.

For anyone who could penetrate beneath the surface, a garden was like a book, full of meaning and of symbols tied in with the beauty of nature. So it was that a man could

read these symbols and gain endless comfort from such a garden.

During the Heian period a refined society watched the seasonal changes in the garden, gazing from the verandah,or from boats with richly carved prows. One of the favourite amusements was the 'ceremony of the winding brooks'. Seated alongside the stream, the courtiers would put their verses into goblets and send them downstream, for their companions to add their rhymes.

The emperor Saga[16)] undoubtedly was responsible for a new trend in garden design. In the year 823 BC he abdicated in order to live out his life on his country estate, in the midst of his garden. The dominant feature of this garden, which has survived to this day, was Lake Ozawa, four square kilometres (one and a half square miles) in extent, with the picturesque Kyoto hills rising beyond. Of the original garden, there are two islands in the lake and stones representing boats prepared to set sail for the island of Horai.

Historical accounts describe this garden in the spring, when the air was full of birdsong and the scent of flowering shrubs. On autumn evenings the moon was reflected from the waters of the lake; Emperor Saga was a connoisseur of Chinese literature and calligraphy, and loved the scenery of his garden so much that he arranged festivities of moon-gazing,

41 *Toshodaiji near Nara; the Chinese abbot T'ien Chen founded the temple and its garden in 759. The Chinese influence can be seen in the use of colour both in the buildings and the garden*

42 *Clipped trees and shrubs, Horyuji, Nara*

together with poetic competitions on such themes as the shadow of the moon on the lake in autumn, with prizes for the successful poets. This delight in the beauty of the moon became an essential element in Japanese culture. Later on 'moon watching verandahs' were constructed jutting over the waters of the lake, and bridges shaped like the new moon, or so constructed that those standing on them could enjoy the reflection of the moonlight in the spray of a waterfall.

The emperor Saga also introduced the Heian nobility to the fashion of 'mountain homes' set in these gardens with lakes. At the same time the Jodo (pure earth) Buddhist sect was building extensive temples near the capital, surrounded by gardens containing lakes. The teachings of the Jodo sect spread rapidly, particularly because unlike other Buddhist sects which taught that each individual had to seek salvation by his own strenuous efforts, Jodo promised rebirth in the blissful Western Heaven to all who confessed the name of Amida Buddha.

The Jodo temple gardens which symbolized the beauties of paradise, were also the scene of aristocratic social life in Heian. These occasions were purportedly religious festivals, but in fact the pleasures offered were worldly and provided a welcome escape from reality, for dark clouds were gathering over the City of Peace and Concord. Poverty and famine wracked the land while political and religious rivalry were rife among the nobility.

43 This painting on a fan captures the atmosphere of a garden of the Heian period; by an unknown painter of the 17th century

44 Boating in a garden of the Heian period. A painting on a fan by an unknown artist of the 17th century

We can still appreciate the setting for these festivities, from the poetic architectonic creation, the Byodoin (Hall of the Phoenix) in Kyoto. It was part of a temple built in the *shinden* style, and the lake was integral to the whole design. Even today it has an enchanting and irresistible beauty.

Favourable circumstances have preserved some parts of the lake gardens of a temple in the far north-east of Japan, in the city of Hiraizumi. In the 12th century, the nobleman Fujiwara Kiyohira, Lord of Motsu, founded a city which was to rival Heian. Fragmentary remains of his gardens correspond to the literary descriptions of landscape gardens in the *Sakuteiki,* and allow us to assume that there was a *shinden* style seat here, with a lake of the seascape type, with stones weathered by wind and waves. What remains is an eloquent testimony to the high standards attained by garden designers so long ago.

The most effective description of the Heian gardens is to be found in the love story *Genji monogatari* (The Tale of Genji) by Lady Murasaki Shikibu [17)], a lady-in-waiting. According to this romance, which reads almost like a modern novel, the garden was the scene of recreation, love, passion, sadness, and the various festivals celebrated throughout the year. She describes the stones, the trees, the lakes and the streams, much as they were later depicted by the illustrators of her romance and by the painters who took their inspiration from her work for decorating fans, screens and other *objets d'art.*

In the chapter of her romance entitled 'The Festival of Flowers', the author describes a banquet arranged by the emperor in Spring, under the flowering cherry tree by the southern courtyard. Although rain was forecast, the weather was wonderful; the sun shone and birds sang in the trees.

45 *A view of the Sanzenin garden in Kyoto. The temple was founded at the end of the 8th century*

The emperor drew lots for rhymes, and all those present composed verses in the Chinese manner. Musicians entertained in the garden, and towards evening the enchanting song, the 'Dance of the spring larks', was performed.

In their exclusive palaces and gardens the Heian nobility created an enchanted world far removed from the reality of the times. It was a world which realized the ephemeral nature of the earth; a world of poetry and bittersweet memories. These nobles led cossetted lives with time to appreciate the essence of beauty. Nature was their inspiration, but not nature alone: it was nature so contrived as to deepen their experience and to make it more intense, to transform it into a lingering nostalgia, full of the strange, indefinable sadness which comes from understanding the transience of life. This melancholy was a cure for their own hard hearts

46 A Heian carriage and garden represented on a woven kimono belt

47 Aoimatsuri in Kyoto; a Heian cart, decorated with flowering wisteria for the festival

and was expressed in the idea of *mono no aware.* In the 18th century the literary critic Motoori Norinaga[18] described this concept as a melancholy sensitivity to things and events; to the falling petals of a flower, to tears that do not fall, to the short-lived beauty of blossom, to the sudden onset of autumn.

Today there are still reminders of these Heian gardens in Japanese life. In Spring there are the cherry blossom festivals, in autumn the search for the beauty of the scarlet maple leaves, and all the year round verses are written in praise of the many beauties of nature.

The Heian art of landscape gardening with its artificial hills, lakes and islands, its careful arrangement of stones, remained part of all later schools of garden design. This unbroken tradition is one of the essential features of Japanese garden art.

48 *A garden scene from* The Tale of Genji, *painted on a paper screen by an unknown 18th-century painter*

49 *This procession, in traditional Heian costume, is a survival of an ancient ceremony held in temple and palace gardens*

上座石

The wise man learns all, without needing to go anywhere; he distinguishes all things, without needing to look at anything.

Lao-tze

A constant inspiration

A golden twilight, carpets of soft moss, tree-trunks mirrored in the surface of a lake, a remarkable harmony of autumn colours, an atmosphere of inner peace and radiance, nature perfected by the hand of man – this is a description of the garden of the Saihoji temple in Kyoto, known also as Kokedera, the Moss Temple. It has been a source of never-failing inspiration since it was founded in the 14th century.

The aim of much Japanese endeavour is that man may somehow merge with nature, that a delimited space can be made to symbolize the course of the universe. For man's creative powers to be liberated as they were in the creation of this garden, there had to be a long history of self-discipline, and mastery of the set order and of the techniques of the craft. Based on this, it became the Japanese tradition to value all that results from long training of the hand and the mind and all that serves the needs of everyday life. Nothing was ever too ordinary for the Japanese to transform it into an aesthetic experience. If they wished to avoid formal stereotypes, this approach taught them to explore beneath the surface of a subject and

51 This grove of bamboos is part of the Saihoji garden, Kyoto

◀ *50 A woodcut print of the Saihoji garden, Kyoto*

52 The moss garden, Saihoji, Kyoto

53 *Rito:* Landscape with a waterfall *(c. 12th century)*

54 *A garden with artificial hills showing the positions of waterfalls and stones (line drawing)*

to discover new aspects — even if it were only the pattern of the grains in a piece of wood or the shadow of a bamboo plant on a white wall.

The classical period for this approach to landscape gardening spanned the 13th to the 15th centuries, a period marked at first by violent social change. Although officially the emperor remained in power, in fact his over-refined imperial court was incapable of exercising that power and let it slip away from the City of Peace and Concord. The military regents settled in far-off Kamakura to be as free as possible from the debilitating influence of the capital, and imposed on the trouble-torn land a regime in accordance with their own principles. In the early years stress was laid mainly on hard work and a sober and frugal lifestyle in sharp contrast to the luxurious, idle and aimless lives of the Heian nobility. Life took on more sober colours, and the longing for peace in the islands of the immortals caused changes to take place.

The teachings of the Zen sect of Buddhism exercised a profound influence on the thought and life of the warriors during this period[19]. Zen Buddhism had been filtered by Chinese thought on its way from India to Japan, and was particularly influenced by Taoism, the poetic antithesis to the rational sobriety of Confucianism[20]. Taoism rejected book-learning as the way to know the world, and made it the goal of human life to 'liberate the soul from vain trivialities' and to become as one with nature.

In the quest for this moment of illumination (*satori*), Zen Buddhism did not rely on verbal communication nor the reading of scriptures, but on control over the emotions and the discipline of mental concentration. These aspects of Zen were very much in keeping with the mentality of the military rulers in Kamakura[21] and of the later shoguns of the Ashikaga family[22]. They adopted Zen as their religion and its influence spread through all spheres of life. It left its most profound and permanent traces, however, in art, where it led to the formation of an original and remarkably mature aesthetic code.

The importance of Zen for art lay primarily in the importance it attached to intuition, liberating the mind from the habitual way of thinking by means of meditating on paradoxes such as a black dog which is white, or clapping of a single hand. This freed a vast and hitherto unknown region of the mind for artistic feeling and vision. The way to this state of mind was not arbitrary, however; it was conditioned by strict discipline and concentration. The pupil had to relinquish his own identity and become submerged in the atmosphere created by the master, eventually to arrive at an understanding of what the master was doing. It often

55 *A waterfall was a regular feature of landscape gardens*

56 *Positioning stones in the garden (woodcut)*

57 *Portrait of Sesshu, painter and garden designer*

took years of silent apprenticeship and abnegation before the pupil learned the basic techniques of his craft, only to spend the subsequent period learning to free himself from their limitations. Then in moments of inspiration he would capture the essence of the universe in a few strokes of the brush, or the infinity of silence in a few lines of verse.

It was a process which brought the rhythm of human life closer to that of nature, and the Japanese therefore did not hesitate to take the physical aspects of nature and recreate them in artistic form. This can be seen in the evolution of garden design between the 12th and 15th centuries.

It can be seen particularly clearly in the period which followed the return of the seat of military government from Kamakura to Kyoto, the former Heiankyo; this marked the beginning of the Muromachi period[23)].

The art of garden design attained great heights during this time; various techniques were evolved and different schools of thought developed.

The aesthetic code and the system of symbols which had developed from Heian principles were clarified and made more exact.

The search for new ways of 'expressing the infinity of nature in a single blade of grass' was furthered by the influence of the *sansuiga* school of Chinese landscape painting. With their restrained means of expression and their masterly shading of the ink from the deepest black to delicate pale grey, these paintings were bound to inspire the Zen artists of Japan. They expressed their own feelings and the fruits of their concentrated meditation by means of nature itself – the play of light, the surface of a stone, the flow of water and seasonal change. At the same time the Zen imagination was drawn to ever more stark simplicity that even the painter's brush could not achieve. Its culmination was in the profoundly symbolic gardens of sand and stone, such as the gardens of meditation at

58 Sesshu: Ama-no-Hashidate *(early 16th century)*

59 *Kei-in Sochiku:* A cottage by a mountain stream *(15th century)*

60 Four elegant pastimes *(detail) by an unknown painter, probably of the 16th century*

Ryoanji and Daisenin in Kyoto.

Japanese garden design had much in common, as far as the methods used were concerned, with that other art form typical of Eastern Asia — calligraphy. The principles which hold true for calligraphy are, in essence, those which the gardener must observe. They stress the need for a well-balanced mind, a pure heart, technical mastery, the observance of accepted forms which are at the same time transcended, the need to preserve one's individuality and to achieve an overall harmony.

The rules were many and as time went on they were further evolved and changed in accordance with the function the garden was to serve. The most important principle, and one which had been in the forefront ever since Heian times and was expressed in the introduction to the handbook *Sagaryu jiten niwa koho hidensho,* was that the garden should 'follow nature'. Only if the garden was in harmony with the forces of nature could it fulfil its main function, which was to protect the house from evil influences. The great danger of planting trees or placing stones at random in a garden was stressed, as was the need to keep the balance between the principles of *in* and *yo.*

This intricate system of rules was an integral part of the Eastern way of life, and had to be taken into account in practically all human activity. The designer of a garden had to be guided by them step by step, as he worked, whether he was a high-ranking monk, an artist, or simple gardener. It called for an approach of such discipline and perseverance that it was difficult for the uninitiated observer to comprehend.

To take an example: in addition to the main division of things, by which most stones belong to the *yo* principle, and water to *in,* stones were

further distinguished according to their shape and the site chosen for them. High, massive stones represented the *yo* principle, while stones at the top of a waterfall, or over which water flowed, came into the sphere of *in*. The Japanese did not allow this system to lead to a stereotyped formality. On the contrary, it became the stepping-stone to ever more varied forms of expression, rooted in a sensitive feeling for shape, structure and colour-tone. A constant preoccupation with artistic detail developed, with creative expression allowed to

61 A three-tiered garden lantern shaped like a pagoda

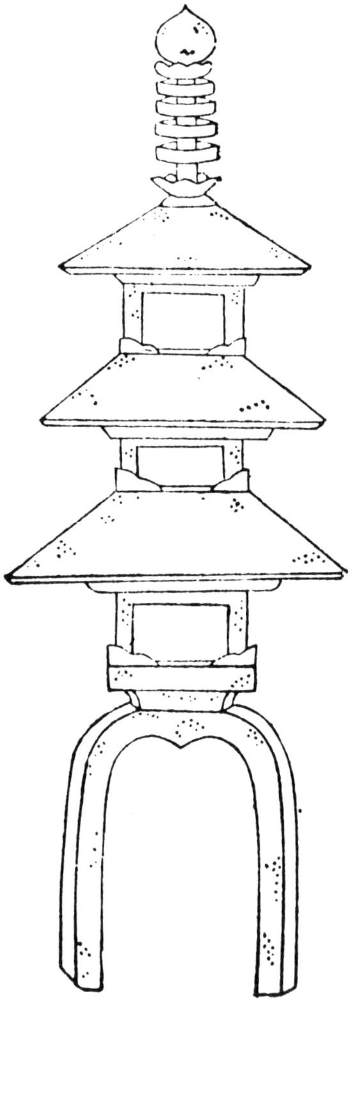

62 A woodcut print of an 18th-century garden lantern

flourish within the framework of the system.

Another part of the garden designer's code was symbolism. This was most marked in the ever more abstract representations of the legends of the island of Horai, the symbolic forms of the tortoise and the crane (emblems of longevity) and of Buddha's disciples (the lohans) represented by stones and compositions of stones. All these elements had become so much a part of the conventional vocabulary of the garden that the merest hint was sufficient to set in motion a chain of ideas and feelings.

The ritual aspect of the garden also had its aesthetic forms. According to the *Secret book of the Saga school of garden design,* besides the principal island the garden also had its 'island of the guest', where a visitor went first of all to bow to the 'guest stone', before going to bow to the ritual stone on the 'island of the master of the house'. From this central island he then looked towards the 'stone protecting the house'. Accompanied by his host he then went to admire the waterfall, or other remarkable features of the garden. When his visit drew to a close he returned to the guest island, bowed once more, and left. In smaller gardens the two side islands were represented by stones dedicated to the master of the house and to the guest. The island of Horai, too, could be represented by a stone.

63 A garden lantern shaped like a pagoda by a stream

64 Night scene in the Shotenin garden by the contemporary painter and graphic artist Taizo Minakawa

The old gardeners' handbooks give the names of the stones used in creating a garden. This was the bible without which it was impossible to design a garden, or to understand the meaning of one. In the garden book *Musoryujiten,* attributed to the most famous garden artist of the day, Muso[25], one hundred and six stones are named and briefly described. The right choice and siting of the stones made it possible for the garden to suggest, with limited means, high mountains, shady valleys, or the sea coast. The book speaks of the 'motionless stone' which was an essential feature of the waterfall; nearby was the 'child stone', and then the 'sun-and-moon-stone' and the 'white cloud stone'. The 'nameless stone' close to the waterfall, broke the direct view to make the stream of water seem longer than it really was. Near the 'island of the master of the house' was the stone 'on which the seagull perches'. Where the stream flowed into the lake there was the 'inlet stone', and in the bed of the stream there were the 'rapids stone', 'the stone beaten by the waves' and the 'stone around which the leaves are whirled'.

Lakes were an important symbolic feature of a garden; in the *Musoryuji-ten* the different shapes are illustrated in brush sketches. There is a lake shaped like the Chinese character for the heart, one shaped like the character for water, and a long narrow lake resembling a brook. The shores of the lakes were formed with little bays and inlets, as found in natural landscapes.

Together with the other components, streams and bridges contributed to the impression of the type of landscape the garden was intended to the present. The foundation of the art was a remarkably exact and sensitive observation of the natural scene, and the experience handed down through many generations. Thus a stream running through mountain scenery was narrow and lined on both sides with groups of stones; the bridge over it was of stone or rough timber. A stream in the plains formed expanses of pure white sand with bushes growing alongside. This would be spanned by an earth bridge, or one made of planks. 'The bridge to Heaven' led towards the mountain tops, and was not intended to be walked over.

Badly placed stones were called the 'stones of poverty, sickness and death', and one had to be careful to avoid them. There were many other interdictions given in the handbooks: it was wrong to build a bridge close to a waterfall, or the island of Horai; the peak of a mountain should not be represented by too sharply pointed a stone, groupings of stones should not be too large, the 'motionless stone' at the top of the waterfall should never be forgotten, and so forth. The code forced the designer to introduce order into the things he used, and led even the less skilled step by step towards goals which would otherwise have remained the province of unusually talented minds.

*

During the Muromachi period, a new type of garden corresponding to a different way of life grew up from the roots of Heian traditions and the influence of Zen Buddhism and northern Sung painters[26]. For the most part the spacious grounds designed by the Heian artists to set off the *shinden* style buildings were no longer available, and the more strictly limited space was seen particularly in the gardens of the *shoin* residences.

66 *The Golden Pavilion, Kinkakuji, Kyoto*

◀ 65 *A pavilion in the Daitokuji garden, Kyoto (woodcut)*

67 *Stones in the lake by the Golden Pavilion*

This name was taken from that of the principal room in the complex of these warriors' homes which was originally a study but later the main hall of the house. A significant feature of the *shoin* was that it opened directly on the modest-sized garden which was designed to be looked at from the house. At this time small, intimate gardens adjacent to the abbot's house were made within the framework of extensive temple gardens. The principal features of Heian gardens, lakes, islands, and streams, were retained in smaller proportions, and in the same way the symbolism of the Heian gardens was perpetuated, based as it was on simple ideas from the distant past, ideas of what can bring happiness to man, and how he can attain a state of benediction. Under the influence of Zen aesthetics, however, the naivety of these ideas was transformed in the search for conciseness into a much more abstract form of expression, far from the simplicity of the original flash of imagination.

The chief purpose of the garden was no longer to be a tranquil setting for leisurely boating on the lake, since the task of digging deep enough for lakes and rivers was too formidable.

68 *One of the entrances to the garden of the Golden Pavilion in Kyoto. Moss combined with paving*

69 *A landscape garden with a pavilion (woodcut)*

The temple garden was intended for walking in, and the winding paths, along which the scenery was expected to be constantly changing, became more important. The paths led the visitor from sunny spaces to shady nooks, and brought him to stand in admiration before compositions in stone. The ground plan of the garden changed; formerly reminiscent of a horseshoe, it now became almost a semi-circle.

The fashion for designing gardens at the foot of mountain slopes led to the new fashion of gardens on several levels, which could be enjoyed from two-storeyed pavilions.

It became more and more popular to enjoy the garden from the verandah of the *shoin,* and this fashion influenced the general design. The impression created was one of nature coming right into the house, and the style led to a number of changes in the rules of composition; for instance, the waterfall was now turned to face towards the *shoin.*

The lake was shallower now that it was not used for boating; it was only on average 60 cm (2 ft) deep. The dominant motifs to which the eyes of the master of the house and his guests were to be drawn were islands and islets in the lake, or groupings of stones. Islands were so designed as to be delightful from whatever side they were viewed. The technique of building stone islands has certain unusual features during this period; the foundation, which was extremely hard, was built of several layers of earth and stones, so that it is possible to date these islands by the technique used. Islands shaped like the tortoise and the crane were still very popular; the tortoise island was usually formed of seven stones, those which symbolized the animal's head, four legs and tail being grouped round the central stone. The head was turned towards

70 Composition of bamboo and stone close to a house

the east, and it was a fashion of the time to plant a pine tree on the tortoise island. Stones representing the bird's wings were a characteristic feature of the crane island.

The pine and the willow were the favourite trees, and there was usually one of them on the central island (*nakajima*). Pine trees were also planted near the artificial hill and the waterfall. Other frequently chosen trees were flowering cherry, maple and plum.

Zen brought a new and important feature into the life of the warriors or *samurai,* the need for meditation. This was met by the temples in the form of carefully designed gardens that induced meditation. These were square or rectangular in plan. The warriors and often the shogun himself lived a semi-monastic life, and spent long hours in these gardens, away from the troubles of the outer world.

The flourishing art of landscape gardening during the Muromachi period was largely due to the shoguns of the Ashikaga family, who took such a delight in garden design themselves that they set the style. Their aesthetic approach was deeply influenced by Zen thought and, indeed, Zen monks enjoyed a privileged position at the Ashikaga court. Abbots of the sect were often the shogun's advisers in economic and political matters, and the Zen temples became the centres of Japanese culture. Contact with China brought new influences to bear after the first shogun of the Ashikaga family, Takauji[27)], abolished the prohibition on trade with Japan's great continental neighbour. The exchange of goods with China was of considerable economic importance for Japan, and helped towards meeting the cost of building the religious centre of the time, the Tenryuji temple.

Trade also brought to Japan large numbers of Chinese paintings and *objets d'art* which were not only greatly admired, both at the shogun's court and at that of the emperor, but were also studied and appreciated.

It was in this connection that the office of *dobo* evolved; the *dobo* were the shogun's companions and artistic advisers, part lay-men and part Zen monks, they were often men of humble origins. At the shogun's court they were held in esteem for their

71 *Bamboo is one of the most characteristic plants of a Japanese garden*

knowledge and ability in the sphere of elegant entertainment, in flower arrangement, and for their knowledge of art and particularly of Chinese paintings and antiquities.

Their position was hereditary and carried with it the title 'ami'. The most famous *dobo,* Noami (1397–1467), Geiami (1431–1485) and S'ami (1472–1525), were father, son and grandson.

The *dobo* were largely responsible for creating the refined atmosphere and the enjoyment of beauty that reigned among the educated Japanese of this period. It grew from the conscious endeavour to penetrate to the very heart of things, the urge for peace, but dynamic, not ultimate stillness. It became the link between

72 *A garden with palms and a stone bridge (woodcut)*

past, present and future, and set men free from the monotonous and inevitable passage of time. The specific quality of this aesthetic attitude was expressed in the concept of *yugen,* which literally means 'mystery'. It was the evocation in a work of art of an atmosphere of mystery, no more than hinted at; a mystery that gave a deeper significance to things, yet itself remained inexpressible.

Brush and ink offered the technique most close to this attitude and

73 *It was in the 16th century that palms became popular in Japanese landscape gardens. This fashion was encouraged by Toyotomi Hideyoshi*

75 *A detail of the door of the Higashi Honganji temple, Kyoto, shows the flowers of the paulownia tree* ▶

74 *Clipped trees and shrubs on sloping ground, Koyasan*

it was by this means that the art of suggestion was developed, empty space becoming of prime significance. Each stroke of the brush expressed an inner force, and transcended the limits of convention. The subject of this art form was nature.

The Japanese painters were for the most part Zen monks, and they studied their art and their creed in China. The Hokuga school of painting emerged from this background, led by Shubun[28], with a number of other first rate landscape painters. Their works depicted distant perspectives shrouded in mist, silhouettes of high mountains, and enchanting nooks where hermits or scholars humbly lived. Of these painters Sesshu[29] contributed notably to the development of garden design. In addition to his delightful landscapes which were taken by gardeners for their inspiration, Sesshu himself designed a number of gardens, of which Joeiji and Unkokukan in Yamaguchi are still in existence.

The shoguns of the Ashikaga family were connoisseurs of northern Sung painting, and this had a marked influence on their love of landscape gardens.

The most influential person in the realm of gardening during this period was Muso Kokushi[30]. He was a Zen abbot who was an intimate friend of the shoguns Takauji and Tadayoshi[31] and spent the last years of his life in Kyoto, where he laid out gardens which have become classics of this Japanese art. The most remarkable is the garden of the Saihoji temple.[32] Like some other famous gardens, it was formed by adapting the garden surrounding the former temple of the Jodo (pure earth) sect. Muso converted the temple to Zen Buddhism, but in his treatment of the garden he drew on and perfected the older traditions. On the site of what is now Saihoji there was already a garden arranged on two levels before Muso arrived. The lower garden was landscaped in the Heian lake garden style and, fundamentally, Muso's garden preserved it as such, although new features can be traced among the old. It is now considered to be a transitional form between the Heian and the later purely Zen designs. It was a garden designed for walking in and had four pavilions. One of them, called Ruriden, stood on an island in the lake and being two-storeyed offered a view of the whole garden. Unfortunately, not one of

these pavilions has survived and Shonantei as it now stands is a reconstruction dating from the Azuchi-Momoyama period[33].

The dominant feature of the lower garden is the long lake, the Golden Lake, shaped like the Chinese character for the heart. It lies north-south, and is broken up by islands. Slender trees bend over the water and are mirrored in the lake, and the shore is broken and irregular, with dark pools and clumps of reeds. Here, too, the traditional symbolism persists: there are the stone tortoise and crane islands in the southern part of the lake, while in the eastern part we see the *yodomariishi,* the 'stones of waiting by night'.

There is a strange charm in this part of the garden, induced by the almost unbroken carpet of moss, which has understandably given its name to the whole garden — Kokedera (the Moss Temple). The mosses form round hillocks, creep over the stones, and climb up the tree trunks, as well as in themselves affording great variety of structure and shades of colour. The sunshine penetrating the branches and foliage of the trees point up their different hues, creating a picture painted by nature and given the finishing touches by a sensitive human hand. Nowhere else in the world, perhaps, has man succeeded in showing the inner values of so modest a plant group as the mosses.

As the slope is mounted colours change to sober greys and browns and the steps lead to the waterfall with no water (Koinzan). Formed of rugged stones, it has been put together with such dynamic force that after gazing at the stones for a while, it seems as though water really is pouring over them, dashing on the rocks below and falling away to carry on more peacefully towards some far-off shore. This all happens in the heart and the mind of the onlooker before his inner gaze, the most reliable compass for human emotions and actions. This was the part of the garden set aside for meditation, and here the soul could loosen its bonds and be born anew to a fresh vision of the world.

The hall of meditation (Shitoan) used to stand here; it was here that the shogun Yoshimitsu[34] used to come to think in peace, and to admire the art of Muso's garden. The eighth in line of the military Ashikaga rulers, Yoshimasa[35], also loved this part of the garden and it was he who eventually saw his family fall from power. Both these shoguns drew inspiration from the beauty of the Saihoji garden, and had gardens similar to it made for their own enjoyment.

It is generally thought that Muso used stones which were already there when he created this stone cascade, and his dry waterfall is thought to be one of the first of its kind in Japan. From the dry waterfall a path led to the top of a hill, from where there is a view of the valley of the river Katsura.

Another of Muso's gardens was the temple garden of Tenryuji[36]. In contrast to the Saihoji garden, Tenryuji carries an atmosphere of radiance, and there are many touches which are of interest to modern landscape

76 The top of a wall: detail showing the arrangement

77 In large temple gardens, walls divide the space into several separate gardens

gardeners. The Zen temple of Tenryuji was founded by the Ashikaga family to give peace to the soul of the dead emperor Go-Daigo[37], whom they had removed from power. It was completed in 1345 and stands on a beautiful spot, with a view of the Arashiyama mountain.

There had already been a temple here in the Nara period, and later, at the end of the Kamakura period, the summer palace of Kamayama, in the *shinden* style, had stood here. There are still traces of this palace to be seen in the garden today.

It is clear that Muso based his design on the original ground plan, and this may be why the garden seems more worldly; the spirit of Heian is still clearly felt. At the same time one cannot fail to note the influence of Sung painting, the inexpressible yet compulsive urge for concision, for the exclusion of the fortuitous in favour of an apposite form of expression. Muso used this approach in garden design with the same resulting harmony as the Chinese painters achieved in their brush drawings.

The garden lies on the northern side of Tenryuji temple, and is meant to be walked in. It has also been designed so that it can be appreciated

from the long verandah of the abbot's rooms. The building is reflected in the lake from which it is divided by a strip of gleaming white sand. The most famous features of the garden are the waterfall, the stone bridge, and the stone islands in the lake.

The waterfall is now a dry stone composition, but originally water did tumble down. It is set against the hillside and the stones which form the watercourse are so placed as to give greater depth to the scenery, as in a Sung painting, and to suggest a greater distance between the waterfall and the hill than in reality.

One feature of the waterfall is particularly characteristic of garden design at this period, and has remained one of the compositional elements used by Japanese gardeners. This is the 'carp stone', or the 'dragon gate' as it is also called. It derives from the Chinese legend that in the upper reaches of the Yellow River there was a great waterfall with three series of rapids, which was an impassable obstacle for all fish swimming upstream. A fish with enough strength and perseverance to move at least a few centimetres upwards, however, was changed into a dragon. Japanese gardeners gave expression to the idea behind the legend by creating a waterfall with a carp stone which appeared to be rising or falling according to the point from which it was viewed – a technique which gives a remarkably dynamic quality to the garden scenery.

We can assume that the Tenryuji waterfall has preserved its original form, as has the most beautiful feature of the garden, the stone bridge. This is made of three carefully chosen flat stones of greenish blue hue. The thickest of these flagstones is the one to the north, which is about 20 cm (8 in) thick, while the middle flagstone is thinner and the third thinner still. It seems clear that the last two flags were split. They are supported on rocks, a technique which was much used later on, probably following the fashion of Tenryuji. It is typical of the Muromachi period that there is no additional arrangement of stones to complete the appearance of the bridge, as was the later custom.

The stone bridge in the Tenryuji garden shows the masterly art of Japanese gardeners, and typifies their skill in observing natural forms and

78 *The garden in the temple courtyard behind the Golden Pavilion*

79 *The garden of the Silver Pavilion in the 18th century (woodcut)*

their ability to choose materials to form a harmonious whole.

The third of the Ashikaga shoguns, Yoshimitsu, was so enchanted by the Saihoji garden that he decided to have one modelled on it for himself. The site he chose was magnificent, surrounded by wooded slopes, where, in the first half of the 13th century there had been a garden of the Heian type with a waterfall and lake 'gleaming like a jewel'.

Here Yoshimitsu built his summer residence, Kitayama, which later became the temple of Rokuonji. It was built in the *shinden* style. Only the three-storeyed Golden Pavilion, Kinkabu, survived, and even this was burned down by an arsonist in 1950. However, it was rebuilt five years later, exactly according to the original plans.

This delicate little building, its charms multiplied by reflection in the waters of the lake, was one storey higher than the original, the Ruriden pavilion in Saihoji, and continued the Heian tradition of Byodoin. At the same time it shows the simpler influences of Zen architecture. The elegant line of the walls is stressed by the use of gold foil, while the curved roof forms an airy crown. The pavilion is set in a garden of the lake type, usually attributed to the painter and garden designer Soami.

The lake was designed for boating, so that the shogun and his friends could admire the beauty of the whole landscape. Yoshimitsu seems to have concentrated on building the pavilion, and only made a few changes to the garden, which is why the Heian features are still so marked.

The islands and the stones arranged in the lake symbolize the legend of Horai, but they are carefully placed so as not to interfere with the reflection of the pavilion in the water. It is a particular charm of the garden that it merges into the wooded hillsides around it. From the top storey of the pavilion there is a most beautiful view of the whole of the garden which gives an impression of being far away from the everyday world; an unforgettable experience.

Over half a century later, shogun Yoshimasa, the grandson of Yoshimitsu, was moved by the Ashikaga

80 *A view of the Silver Pavilion — Ginkakuji — showing the conical pile of sand, Kyoto*

family love for gardens and the leisure hours spent there to build a summer residence for himself at the foot of Mount Higashiyama. Like his grandfather, Yoshimasa admired and often visited the Saihoji garden, and his fascination with it soon led him to want a similar garden of his own. There was yet another reason, derived from the young shogun's filial affection; it was his wish that his mother should also be able to enjoy at least a reflected image of the beauty of Saihoji, for as a woman she could never see the original. Women were not allowed beyond the temple walls, and no exception was made even for so exalted a family as the Ashikagas.

Old records testify that Yoshimasa began to consider a suitable place for his garden very early, in 1465, but his plans for a quiet life in seclusion were upset by the disturbances in the country, which heralded the fall of his family. It was 1482 before he was able to make his dream a reality, in a place of trees and flowing with water.

In the course of the first year progress with his villa, modelled on the Ruriden pavilion in Saihoji, was fast, but then lack of money slowed things down. Some of the buildings, but not all of them by far, were completed during the next three years. Only then did work start on the garden, and rocks and trees were brought to the site. However, the shogun did not live to see his dream perfected, for he died in 1490 at the age of fifty-five. In accordance with his wish, the residence was turned into a temple, and was given the name of Jishoji.

The upheavals which brought the country to civil war after the shogun's death ruined the temple, which was looted by soldiers. It was not until the early 17th century, when Japan was again united under the Tokugawa family[38], that the temple was restored and the lake cleared. The garden was not restored to its original appearance, however, and there are many features of a later date.

We do not know who really designed the garden, but it is very probable that the famous garden artist Soami, who created many of the gardens of Kyoto, also had a hand in landscaping Yoshimasa's garden.

The lake is the characteristic feature of the garden, and in it is reflected the Silver Pavilion – so called because the shogun may have intended it to be adorned with silver foil, although it never was. He is known to have loved the colour, which is the colour of moonlight. The line of the roof of the Silver Pavilion is reminiscent of the Golden Pavilion, and so is the ground plan, but the treatment of the building itself is different. The ground floor is arranged for living in, with sliding walls to the rooms, so that the living space is more closely bound to the lake than is the case in the Golden Pavilion. The first floor was designed in the then fashionable 'Chinese' style known as Kara-yo, with windows resembling those of a temple.

There are Heian-style islands in the lake. Some of the arrangements of stones bear signs of treatment typical of the Muromachi period, while others clearly date from much later, when the garden was restored. One of the features dating from the Muromachi period is undoubtedly Hikkakudo, the Island of the White Crane (even though the name itself dates from the Meiji period[39]), in front of Yoshimasa's study; other Muromachi items include some of the stone compositions, and two stone bridges leading to the tortoise island. These have retained a rustic simplicity and are made of flagstones in the style of the bridge in the Tenryuji temple garden. The waterfall with the 'pond where the moonlight bathes' is justly famous, but the deepest impression is made by two creations in white sand, by the Silver Pavilion. Their gleaming whiteness is in striking contrast to the rest of the garden, with the humid atmosphere of the lake and the dark shadows of the trees.

The first of these compositions in white sand is a plateau about 60 cm (2 ft) high, the surface of which is raked in lines representing the waves of the sea glinting in the moonlight. It is called Ginshadan (literally, silver sand waves). The other feature is a conical structure about 1.8 m (6 ft) high, with a flat top. It is called Kogetsudai (moon-viewing terrace).

It is not known exatly when or how these compositions came into being, but it seems probable that they are a product of the Japanese talent for giving an aesthetic appeal to what would in other circumstances remain a prosaic heap of sand left lying round after the garden was finished. Some scholars believe that they were created at the same time as the garden, and the shogun's love of watching the moonlight would seem to support this view.

In daytime this stretch of carefully raked sand, the treatment of which, as we see from old records, has changed several time in the course of the centuries, comes as a strange and gleaming surprise, while on moonlit nights it evokes silence and sensations of sadness and mystery. Essentially, however, it concentrates the mind and that was undoubtedly the intention of the Zen-inspired artist who created these strange symbols, whoever he may have been.

81 The dry garden landscape of the Silver Pavilion showing the expanse of raked sand

82 *A dry garden landscape in the Nijo garden, Kyoto*

To stay still . . . and take no action.
From the anthology of Zenrinkushu

Dry gardens

Imagine creating a garden with a waterfall, a stream and an expanse of sea, all without a single drop of water and in a space of, say, less than a few dozen square metres bounded by a clay wall or a hedge. This is such an essentially Japanese idea that in itself it could stand as the symbol of the very nature of Japanese culture.

Dry gardens are the outcome of the Zen practice of clearing the mind through long hours of meditation, 'wandering with no goal', in a world of silence and complete spiritual freedom. Such gardens are a strange and unique realization of philosophical ideas on an aesthetic plane. It is not their purpose to create an inspiring atmosphere by means of an overwhelming abundance of beauty, colour and form, but by the opposite means – by suggestion and refined simplicity. It is as if their creators had set up signposts pointing to innumerable paths rather than stating a clear direction. This type of aesthetic thinking transfers the emphasis from form to the undercurrents of life which have no limits and spread into infinity like waves across the sea.

Society in medieval Japan was fettered by conventions which controlled all aspects of human life, even the emotions, and this aesthetic approach presented an opportunity to gain an inner freedom and room for individual thought.

Karesansui – dry gardens – evolved mainly in the Zen temples. Their style became clearly defined in the second half of the Muromachi period, although the term *karesansui* had

83 *Rocks arranged along the bank of the lake in the Nijo garden, Kyoto*

84 Jagged cliffs on the coast often inspired the designers of landscape gardens

already been used in the earliest known handbook for gardeners, the *Sakuteiki.* Here, however, it would appear to have a different meaning; in the Heian gardens with their many lakes and watercourses, it would seem to have referred to that part of the garden where there were only trees and bushes and no water. This is based on what we can deduce from the pictorial material available. The term *karesansui* was used later in a different sense.

Since the gardeners' handbooks were primarily records of an oral tradition, phonetically identical characters were often interchanged: instead of *kare* (dry) the character for *kara* (Chinese – literally T'ang, after the dynasty of that name) was sometimes used. In the medieval gardeners' handbook *Tsukiyama sansuiden* we already find plans for making a dry garden, and *karesansui* is given here under the name *karamizugata,* as one of the seven types of garden. In the handbook *Tsukiyama teizoden*[40], dating from the first half of the 18th century, there are illustrations showing what a dry garden should look like, and how the stones should be arranged. There are also notes on how to use sand, shrubs and grasses. One of the illustrations is a sketch from memory of the famous dry garden of Ryoanji[41], here described as a level sand garden (*heisha*).

By this time the dry garden had its

rightful place among other Japanese gardening styles; it was no longer confined to temple gardens, but was also to be found in those magnificent garden complexes surrounding the homes of the nobility.

The development of modern architecture has made the dry garden famous throughout the world, and so it has become the bond between two very different worlds — the world of Zen silence and the great modern cities, noisy but longing for peace, nevertheless.

It is very likely that in the first place necessity led to the idea of the dry garden. In the distant past there had already been temples in the capital whose grounds did not enjoy the abundant water supply needed for a traditional garden. In order to supply the essential element of water in their gardens the monks may have had to resort to creating a symbolic waterfall or dry lake. Sudden tectonic changes in a land so stricken by earthquakes as Japan may also have caused springs to dry up, and thus revealed to the Japanese, with their remarkable perception of beauty, the unique charm of a dry stream bed, the form and inner value of stones and pebbles washed for years or even whole centuries by flowing water. 'False' dry gardens, where the water disappeared due to some such catastrophe, are still carefully preserved in Japan, and arouse the same admiration as the magnificent interior of an outwardly simple lacquer box, or the rich and flamboyant elegance of the lining to a plain robe.

It must also be borne in mind that the making of artificial streams and lakes in gardens led to great progress

85 *Such a natural landscape could serve as a model for a garden design*

in gardening techniques, as can be seen from research into old Japanese gardens, or what remains of them. Japanese gardeners explain the word *kawaracho* (gardener) as meaning literally 'he who makes the beds for streams'; it was one of the most important tasks in the composition of a Japanese garden.

To place a symbolic stream or waterfall in a garden without water was made possible by a very detailed gardeners' code which was already formulated by the end of the 12th century. This code determined and gave names to the stones which were to be used when building a waterfall, rapids or a brook flowing into a lake. It also laid down the general outline of the islands to be built, the line to be followed by the banks of stream, the shape of bridges according to the type of landscape the garden was to represent. It gave a structure of lines and forms such as would be sketched by the painter's brush. But unlike the brush drawings of the Chinese and Japanese masters, which evoked nature, the garden was at one with nature — ever changing and at the same time offering a clue to further discovery. To attain the Zen ideal of 'emptying' the mind one had to 'stay still and take no action', to free oneself from the routine ways of thinking and set out on a pilgrimage of the spirit during which a dry stream bed in the garden might again murmur with water and the splash of waves, and the soul could pass from the confined space of the temple garden to the inaccessible loneliness of mountain heights or to the sea shore.

The earliest known example of a garden of meditation is Koinzan, the dry garden of the Saihoji temple. In other such gardens, where natural conditions were not so favourable as in Saihoji, a dry landscape was created in a much smaller space, usually square or rectangular in design. There Japanese gardeners proved that there is always sufficient space and opportunity to create a suitable environment for the liberation of man's thoughts.

The best-known dry gardens are those of the temples of Daisenin[42] and Ryoanji. The Daisenin dry garden continues the Horai traditions of previous periods, creating new approaches, whereas the Ryoanji garden, with its conception of absolute simplicity, has never been surpassed by later gardens of meditation.

86 Detail of the stone garden of Ryoanji, Kyoto

87 A dry garden, no trees, no water, just raked sand and fifteen stones; Ryoanji, Kyoto

88 The Ryoanji garden is a place which inspires meditation

Daisenin is one of the *tassho,* the small subsidiary temples of the greater Daitokuji[43] temple. From the east and north sides a dry garden comes right up to the low verandah of the abbot's house but at a slightly lower level. It was probably laid out at the beginning of the 16th century, soon after the monastery was built. The garden is surrounded by a wall and divided by a partition with a lotus-shaped window which frames a view of the entire garden.

In a mere hundred square metres (120 square yards) the unknown designer has created, without a single drop of water, the illusion of a landscape, using only a few strangely broken stones of various sizes, the sober green of a few trees and shrubs and rough sand. However, in the imagination can be seen a spring rising deep in the mountains and rushing over a waterfall to fill the bed of a narrow mountain stream spanned by a small bridge and bordered by jagging cliffs. Stones symbolizing the tortoise and the crane island lie in the bed of the stream, which gradually widens as the water 'foams' over rapids and the surrounding hills become lower and more rounded; the

89 *The stones in the Ryoanji garden are surrounded by strips of moss providing the only note of green in the garden*

stream becomes a river and at last is lost in the white sand of the ocean. A boat floats downstream, bound for the 'island of eternal beatitude'.

According to another interpretation, the stream of water is the unremitting stream of life, and the stone a dead man who is trying in vain to go against the stream. The three sections of the garden are also sometimes taken to symbolize the mystery of creation, human life and the end of life. Another interpretation is that they are symbols of the monastic life: work, meditation and illumination.

The ingenious gardening techniques used have succeeded in giving great depth to the landscape in this very limited space, principally by placing larger stones in the foreground and smaller ones further back. The trees in the background have been trimmed to create a continuous line of greenery, while the shrubs in the foreground have been allowed to retain their natural shapes.

The largest stone in the composition forming the waterfall is 2.2 m (7 ft) high, while the 'motionless stone' nearby is 30 cm (1 ft) lower. They are both so close to the verandah that they seem to be within touching distance and one of the stones in the bed of the stream is placed on a level with the floor of the room. The integration of garden and interior is absolute; the two elements are interwoven, and form a unity.

The gardener who placed these stones in so small a space could not risk a single mistake. From this point of view, too, the Daisenin garden became a model for later Japanese gardeners. All the elements in the composition have a single profound but unexpressed significance.

The Daisenin garden was inspired by the techniques of Chinese brush and ink painting, but at the same time it reveals the very Japanese urge to transform everyday surroundings into a work of art which needs constant nurturing by human hands for its continued existence. It was neither a copy of a painting nor a copy of nature. It was a realization of the same vision which inspired Chinese and Japanese painters of brush and ink landscapes to master the art of merely hinting at an idea or event; the art of what the Zen thinkers called 'playing on a lute with no strings'.

A long tradition of the art of gardening and of highly developed skills were important conditions for the success of such an undertaking. The careful choice of stones, their placing along the dry bed of the stream, the planting of shrubs and trees — all this is the fruit of long experience by a people fascinated by the beauty of nature.

The author or authors of the Daisenin garden left no written record, apparently intentionally. This is in accordance with Zen philosophy where even a single word, once written down, can become a dogma preventing independent thought, concentration and the intuitive recognition of truth.

90 *Taizo Minakawa:* The Stone Garden, *Ryoanji*

91 *Traditional patterns for raking sand in dry gardens. Contemporary drawing by Nihon Bijitsu*

The peak of Zen gardening was achieved in the abbot's garden in the Ryoanji temple of Kyoto, which was built at the very beginning of the 15th century. The famous stone garden, however, was laid out much later, probably at the end of the 16th century. It has been traditionally attributed to the Ashikaga painter and aesthete, Soami, but this has now been disproved.

However, the Ryoanji garden is unmistakably one of Japan's greatest treasures, and makes a profound impression on even the uninitiated, chance visitor. It is so simple, so perfectly dignified, that it seems to be a natural phenomenon.

The garden ground plan is rectangular, with the whole of one long side adjacent to the abbot's verandah. Visitors still take off their shoes, in Japanese fashion, before stepping on to the polished boards of the verandah to spend a while in meditation or admiration of this work of art created centuries ago.

The garden is surrounded on three sides by a clay wall topped with pantiles. This forms a frame for a composition in stone and sand. Within the frame all is harmony in tones of grey and white, shades determined by nature, but subtly changing in rain or sunlight, at dawn or at twilight.

The garden covers an area of 340 square metres (410 square yards), and within this space there are fifteen stones arranged in groups of five, two, three, two and three. The rough stones seem at the same time to move away from the natural clay wall and to come closer again. No stone stands alone; each one has one or two smaller companions. If we look at the groups of stones carefully we feel there is an invisible bond between them, as though they want to draw closer together.

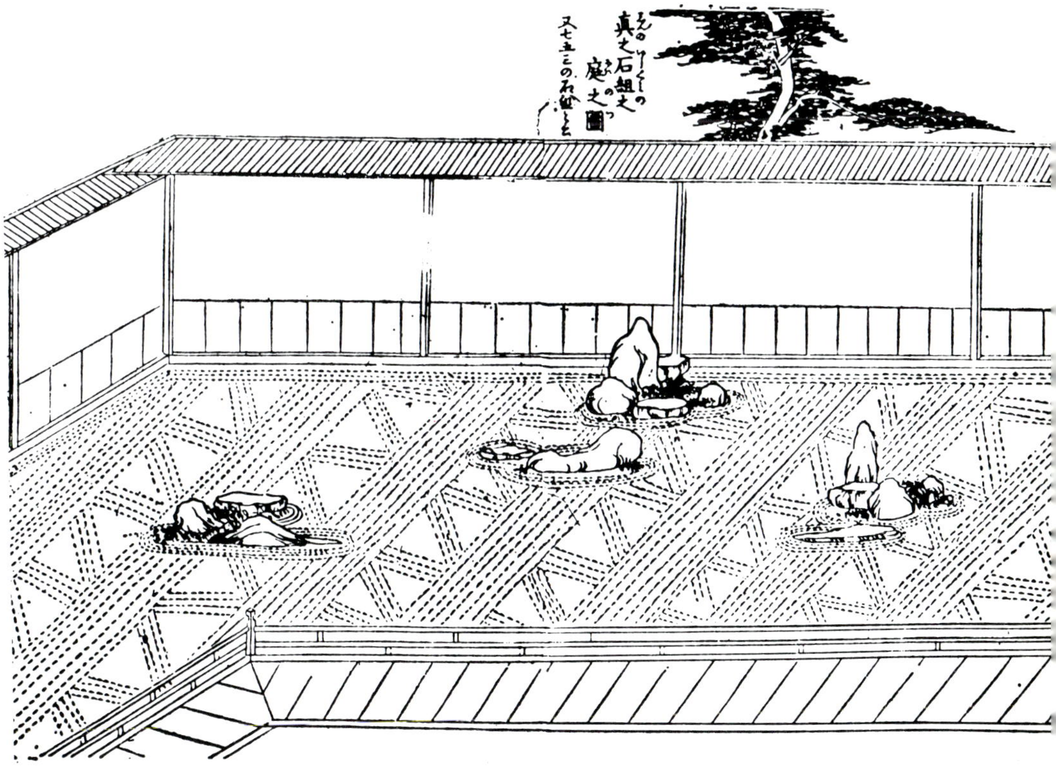

92 *Raking sand round stones in circular or elliptical patterns gives the impression of water breaking against rocks*

93 *Stones arranged in groups of seven, five and three, in the style of Ryoanji (woodcut)*

94 Conical piles of sand; a dry landscape in the abbot's garden, Daisenin, Kyoto

Round the base of each stone there is a narrow strip of moss – the only greenery in the garden. The sand is raked in parallel lines symbolizing waves, while circles and ellipses in the sand round the stones represent the checking of the flowing water.

The garden at Ryoanji is timeless and unbounded; it symbolizes the endless rhythm of the waves and the lightness of the clouds. The language of motionless stones expresses the intense inner feelings of the artist.

What did the creator of this garden want to express? Everything and nothing. That is perhaps a better answer than wondering whether the stones symbolize 'a family of tigers swimming against the current', or 'the islands of eternal beatitude'. For one onlooker the stones may suggest one thing — mountain peaks lost in mist, or a fleeting dream materialized — for another it may mean something quite different. The artist's inspiration will always remain an enigma, as he himself suggested when he left one of his fifteen stones hidden from the eyes, invisible from any point on the verandah. At just such a moment of realization, perhaps, the echo of his quiet laughter floats by, the response to all our guesses. There is a mystery in his garden which never fails to inspire and its tranquility is eternal.

The dry gardens of Daisenin and Ryoanji were the influence behind many similar compositions. Most of these retained the rectangular ground plan enclosed by a wall or hedge. Kyoto is a treasury for such gardens.

One interesting type of dry garden is at the Ryugenin temple, one of the subsidiaries of the great Daitokuji temple. Most of the ground in this garden is covered by continuous waves of moss, in which fairly small stones are set, with azaleas planted close by. The impression created is one of cliffs washed by ocean waves. This elegant garden laid out in the Muromachi period also shows the influence of the traditions of Sung painting.

One of the best known dry gardens in Kyoto is by the abbot's house in the Nanzenji temple[44], traditionally attributed to Kobori Enshu[45]. Most of the space in this garden, which is only slighter larger than the one at Ryoanji, is covered with white sand, with a composition of stones and shrubs along the wall. A few stones placed further in the sand look like islands in the open sea.

Some of these dry gardens are of particularly harmonious colour associations, like that in the Entsuji temple gardens in Kyoto which has an

95 The bushes and trees are trimmed to harmonize with the stones alongside the garden paths, Daisenin, Kyoto

interesting arrangement of fairly low stones alongside the green of the hedge.

An interesting new technique in dry gardens was introduced during the Edo period. Instead of stones, groups of bushes, carefully trimmed, were sometimes placed on the expanse of sand. The abbot's garden in Shodenji[46] is one example of this style. Bushes have been planted along the wall; the tallest bush is 2.2 m (7 ft) high, while the lowest gives the impression of a flat stone and is only 18 cm (7 in) high. The flowing lines they form are emphasized by the expanse of white sand. It is a garden in the Ryoanji style, the only difference being that here there is not a single stone.

In some gardens the only adornment of the flat stretch of sand are conical heaps of sand (*shinzanshiki*). This is the case at Daisenin and the abbot's garden at Myoshinji[47], where the conical piles of gravel have been placed on an expanse of fine white sand.

The aesthetic effect of the dry gardens was attained with the help of detailed instructions. In particular these pertained to methods of representing an expanse of still water and flowing water.

As the preceding descriptions have suggested, an expanse of sand or fine gravel was used to represent still water. In Kyoto, white river sand was commonly used for this purpose. Special wooden rakes were used to draw out patterns on the sand; different rakes were used according to the effect required. The patterns produced by these rakes are known as *hokime,* 'the eye of the rake'. In gardens where a solemn atmosphere is

96 This path in the Daisenin temple garden is paved in the formal shin *style*

97 *The shapes and the surfaces of specially chosen stones attract attention. They are to be seen at the entrances to temples and private homes*

desired the pattern is one of straight lines (*sazaname*), sometimes alternating with bands of plain sand.

Besides straight lines, there are patterns of wavy lines, bent lines, twisted lines. The most complicated design is that of 'waves of the blue sea', in which left- or right-hand spirals suggest rippling water near a stone, just as circles or ellipses are also used.

Since the patterns traced on the sand are easily disturbed by rain or wind, they must be constantly attended to. Visitors to these dry gardens sometimes have the good fortune to see this being done, always by a gardener in traditional dress. They manage the rake with unshakeable skill, never deviating in the slightest from the appointed lines, and leaving no trace of their own footprints in the sand.

The dry stream bed is usually formed of pebbles the size of a man's fist; black pebbles give a particularly elegant effect. A swift mountain stream is symbolized by water-worn pebbles and rough banks.

The shaping of trimmed trees and bushes is an important aspect of dry garden design. It is a means of giving the scenery greater depth. Clipped trees – usually conifers or evergreen trees – may symbolize compositions of stone, or natural forms such as the waves of the sea. The techniques of trimming, developed during the

98 *A composition of stones, trees and shrubs, Daisenin, Kyoto*

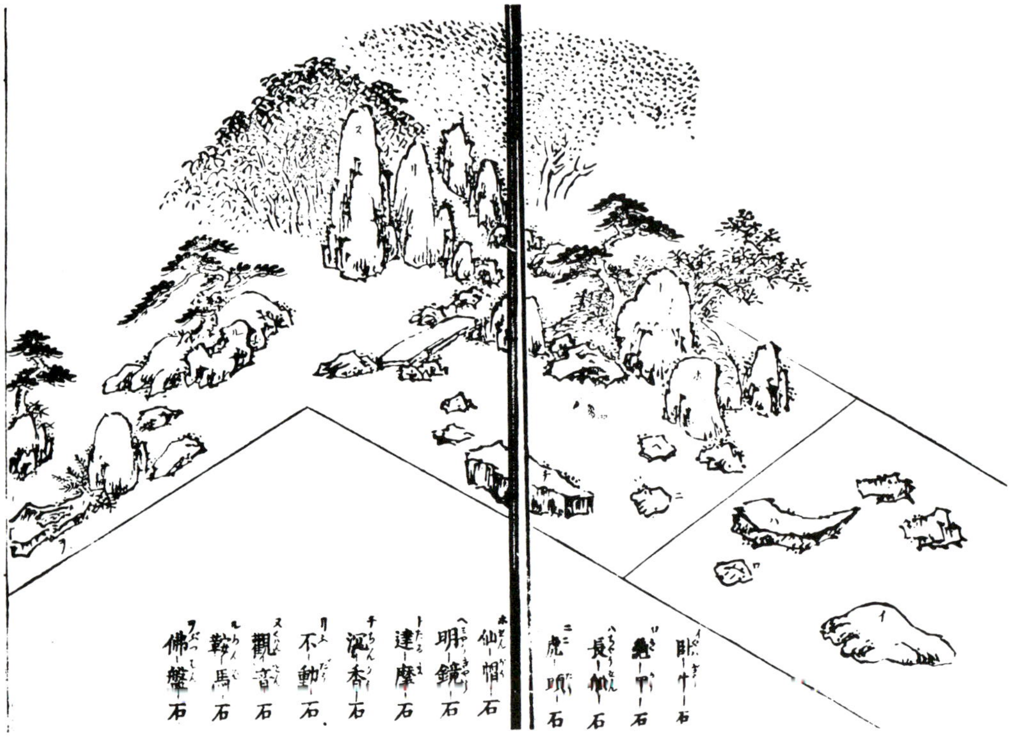

99 *The stone garden of Daisenin, Kyoto (woodcut)*

101 *Detail of a stone composition, Daisenin, Kyoto*

100 *Taizo Minakawa:* The stone garden of the Daisenin temple, *Kyoto*

Momoyama period, became of particular importance from the middle of the 18th century onwards.

Today there are dry gardens all over Japan, many of them new. They are not only found as part of a larger garden, but individually and in public places.

In 1939 Mirei Shigemori designed a remarkable dry garden for the Komyoin shrine of the Tofukuji temple. The garden is surrounded by a hedge and three-quarters of the enclosed space is covered by white sand, with stones to symbolize the shore.

Some of the modern stone gardens designed by such architects as Kenzo Tange, Sutemi Horiguchi and others, form an integral part of the urban planning of the great cities of Japan.

With their simplicity of line, harmony of colour, and the fact that they place no bounds on creative imagination, dry gardens seem made for modern architectural design. In this sphere the traditions of the Japanese gardener's art perhaps make their greatest contribution to a more aesthetic treatment of our environment today.

102 A window in the partition dividing two parts of the garden, Daisenin garden, Kyoto

103 *Another view of the partition with a window dividing the garden of Daisenin, Kyoto*

104 *The last section of the dry garden, Daisenin, Kyoto*

105 A path of tobiishi *set in moss*

A fallen leaf
returning to the twig?
A butterfly fluttering.
Moritake

A haven of peace – the tea garden

If we consider the traditional arts of Japan, their perfect simplicity, their extraordinary talent for abstraction and imagination, we focus on the history of the *chado*, the tea paths, better known as *chanoyu* or the tea ceremony[48].

This is the central point of Japanese culture influencing the arts of architecture, gardening, pottery, calligraphy, painting, flower arranging and others. So for this reason it is important to understand something about the tea ceremony and its history.

Although the ceremony as we know it today is more of a cultivated social occasion than a profound philosophical experience, it nevertheless remains an important social event for Japanese from all walks of life. Therein lies its great contribution to the national culture.

The main principles of the tea ceremony grew out of aristocratic amusements which came to Japan from China during the Sung dynasty, between the 12th and the 14th centuries. These were the tea games or competitions (*chatsuki*), which took

106 *A composition with stones in the garden of the Hoshunin temple which dates from 1608, Kyoto*

107 *The tea house and garden of the 'Study by the Jade River' (woodcut)*

108 *This gate with its thatched roof and the fence in the Kyoto style are characteristic of the good taste of the masters of the tea ceremony, Katsura, Kyoto*

110 *The tea ceremony originally took place in temples; one such place was the Donkaku, part of Hoshunin temple, Kyoto*

109 *Plan of a temple tea garden (woodcut)*

place at the magnificent courts of the emperor and the shoguns and afforded a popular opportunity for social intercourse.

The tea games took place in the most sumptuous hall of the palace, and the religious motif was represented by three scroll paintings from the life of the Buddha Shakyamuni. The room was adorned with choice works of art, of which Chinese brush and ink landscapes were particularly admired. Those taking part in the games were placed according to rank, and each received ten tastes of four different teas. Later the number was enlarged. From the flavour and the fragrance of each they had to guess

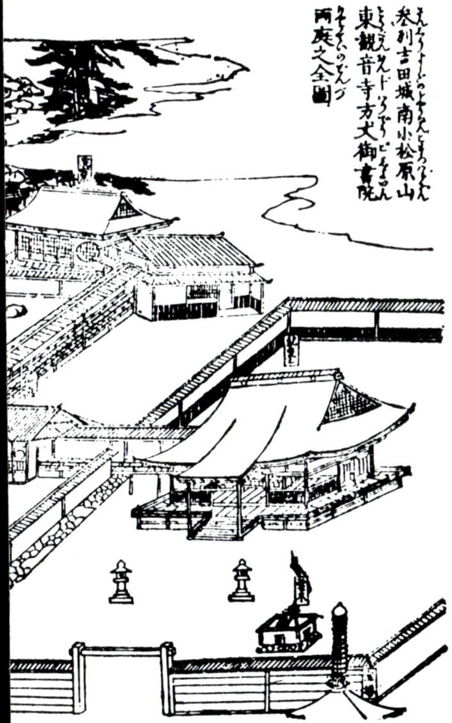
参州吉田城南小松原山
東観音寺方丈御書院
両庭之全図

111 Tobiishi *in front of the Yugetsukan tea pavilion in the Shugakuin garden, Kyoto*

the name of the tea and the place where it was grown. The victor was rewarded and highly praised, and the games culminated in costly festivities.

Amongst the samurai families this social event took on a more specific form. By the end of the Muromachi period an exact code had been drawn up, governing the way in which the rooms were to be decorated and the behaviour of those taking part. Particular attention was paid to the utensils for the ceremony, especially the pottery bowls from which the tea was drunk. In fact appreciating the beauty of each object became an important part of the ceremony.

Tea-drinking became popular

among all classes of people and played a significant role throughout Japan. As Kenzo Tange noted, among the peasants, meeting to drink tea was often the cover for conspiracy, while for the *nouveaux-riches* it was one way of holding their own with those who were more privileged by birth.

Under the influence of Zen Buddhism a new form of the tea ceremony evolved from this broad background. The ceremony then became a specific form of social intercourse for those who wished to revive their senses, dulled by everyday life, through short periods spent in an atmosphere of beauty, harmony and quiet.

This desire was very understandable in a time of war, general havoc, and political intrigue — to which even the famous master of the tea ceremony, Sen no Rikyu[49)], fell victim. Anyone who took part in public life was in constant danger. It was against this background, and under the influence of Zen Buddhist philosophy, that the strange, quiet yet highly emotional drama of the tea ceremony evolved.

Several generations of tea masters and aesthetes of the standing of Murata Shuko[50)], Sen no Rikyu, Kobori Enshu and others, made the tea ceremony into an experience which purified the mind of selfish ambition and vain desire. Those taking part attained such a state of relaxation and inner peace that they were able to appreciate with all their senses the beauty of the simplest things.

The masters of the tea ceremony drew their inspiration for the setting of the ceremony, and its utensils, from the simple cottages of the peasants and fishermen. They rightly appreciated as works of art the objects produced by these folk. This was a reaction against the earlier luxury of tea-drinking in aristocratic circles, and represented a fundamental change in Japanese taste.

The tea ceremony was a drama directed in masterly fashion by the host and given its finishing touches by the guests — the actors. Within this framework there matured an art in which the Japanese are still masters — that of creating an atmosphere by the choice of details so subtle and so sophisticated, that it can only be appreciated by someone who is thoroughly initiated into this whole way of thinking. It has become so much a part of Japanese life that even today

112 A classical tea garden, showing the path of tobiishi, *Katsura, Kyoto*

the creation of the correct atmosphere is naturally considered an important part of every social occasion, both within the family circle and on a wider scale.

The role of the host in the tea ceremony was developed to an extraordinary degree and this in an aspect which is still integral to the Japanese way of life. The host does not need to overwhelm his guests with luxury, but should surround them with ingenious and unobtrusive thoughtfulness and tact. The guest is then called upon to assume his role by the sensitive way he reacts to his host's attentions, thus revealing their full significance.

Here one of the traditional Japanese aesthetic principles, that of *wabi*[51)], plays a fundamental role. *Wabi* is a term which lends itself more readily to explanation than to

114 The way to the tea house (woodcut)

113 In the great gardens of the aristocracy the treatment of the roofs of the tea house and over tops of the garden gates was inspired by peasant architecture, Katsura, Kyoto

115 Woodcut showing a tea house and waiting room for guests; note how the garden is divided up by bamboo fences, hedges and walls

translation by a single word. It is a combination of several complex feelings — a sense of moderation, of inner joy stemming from the choice of simplicity and poverty, and of a calm sadness and apology for the inexorable pattern of life.

It has always been the purpose of the tea ceremony to express these emotions on an aesthetic plane. For it must be remembered that during the Middle Ages the people who took part in the tea ceremony lived in great luxury, so that the realization of *wabi* introduced an important element of self-discipline into their social life. One of the early Japanese poets wrote that *wabi* can be experienced by one who not only appreciates the magnificence of the cherry blossom and of the rich red autumn colour of the maple, but above all has such complete inner harmony that he can enjoy the apparently uninspiring view of the roof of a poor fisherman's hut on the seashore in the autumn twilight. It was in this atmosphere, then, that the very Japanese institution of the tea ceremony evolved.

As early as the 15th century, tea houses were built for lovers of the ceremony[52]. In times of political disturbance the tea house became the place where ostentation and worldliness were replaced by more profound and permanent values, and where spiritual calm and a closer integration with nature could be sought.

According to Sen no Rikyu's ideas, the tea house should evoke the atmosphere of a hermitage deep in the mountains[53]. Rikyu was so thoroughly consistent in his insistence on 'hermit's tea' that it was one of the reasons why he lost favour with the military ruler of the country, Hideyoshi[54], and in accordance with the custom of the time, was forced eventually to take his own life.

With the popularity of the tea ceremony a new and extremely important style of garden design developed — that of *roji* (the tea garden). *Roji* literally means 'path', but when used in the sense of 'tea garden', the first character in the word is that which represents 'dew', not 'path' (both being read in the same way). This implies a subtle shift into the poetical and philosophical sphere. For under

116 This gate with its thatched roof shows the influence of the soan *style of tea ceremony*

117 A hanging garden lantern under the eaves of the house, with a water basin of the chozubachi *type (woodcut)*

118 A water basin of the chozubachi *type is frequently found in tea gardens*

Buddhist influence the Japanese linked dew with the idea of the ephemeral nature of the world and of human life, while at the same time it was bound up with the curious nature of *wabi* which influenced the whole art of the tea garden.

In the history of Japanese gardens the tea garden was the first garden style designed both as a whole and in its component parts for a practical purpose, although this purpose was, of course, bound up with the aesthetic and philosophical character of the tea ceremony. This practical aspect brought the art of the Japanese garden so close to the needs of everyday life that the tea garden was one of the decisive factors leading to the

119 A low water basin of the tsukubai *type with its bamboo scoop*

conception of the residential garden as we know it today.

The principal function of the tea garden was to provide a tranquil setting for the tea ceremony. The modest proportions of the garden allowed the designer to concentrate on each of its component parts right down to the smallest detail, and to bring all into complete harmony.

According to Rikyu the surroundings of the tea house ought to suggest a forest deep in the mountains, with a deserted temple and an almost inaccessible hamlet to be imagined nearby. That was why at first trees from the plains were never planted in tea gardens, nor was it usual to clip or trim the trees in anyway. The other components of the garden – the stones laid along the path, the water basin and the lamp – were intended to contribute to the general atmosphere by their look of weathered age. It was important that the line between nature and the work of human hands should disappear, and that the artist should conceal his art, rather than present it for admiration.

The garden set the tea house apart from the outside world, and for this reason it was not usual to include 'borrowed scenery' (the landscape outside the garden) in the garden design, as was the case in several other styles of Japanese gardening.

There is an interesting story told in this connection, about Rikyu's tea garden in the town of Sakai. The garden lay on the slope of a hill above the sea. When it was ready, Rikyu invited the first guests. To their surprise, the master had planted trees and bushes that hid the view of the sea. Not until a little later, as they bent over the water basin and caught the sparkle of the waves in a gap between the trees did they appreciate the master's intention. He wanted them to understand how close

a bond there is between the drops of water in the basin and the infinite ocean. The art of leaving something still to be discovered was called 'the artist's flower' and it was the task of the guests to discover this 'flower' and thus become a contributing factor to the work of art themselves.

Before the tea ceremony the invited guests meet at the garden gate, at the 'outer waiting-room' with its simple bench. There are two flat flagstones in front of this bench, a smaller one for the chief guest, chosen with particular care, and a larger one for the rest. In the waiting-room of the Yabunouchi tea garden in Kyoto the undemocratic tradition of the days before Rikyu still survives, and there is a special bench for noble guests, spread with matting, while ordinary guests sit on a plain wooden bench. As a rule there are no more than five guests at the tea ceremony because the tea house is very small.

The guest passes into a different world as he goes through the gate to the tea garden. Here inside he leaves

120 *A water basin, filled with sand for the winter, Katsura, Kyoto*

121 *A square water basin in a tea garden, with the traditional bamboo water pipe*

the path, laid with stones. What craftsman's skill and artist's imagination those Japanese gardeners expended on stones whose task is to bear the weight of human footsteps, can only be appreciated by the true connoisseur and lover of the art. Each single stone in the path is carefully selected, and its exact placing is intended to shape the path to the rhythm that the artist wishes to give the visitor's progress.

In Rikyu's conception the tea garden path wound gently like a footpath in the mountains. On the other hand, the masters of the tea ceremony Furuta Oribe[55] and Kobori Enshu introduced straight lines into garden architecture. Rikyu believed the tea path should be six parts useful and four parts beautiful, while Oribe inverted this proportion in favour of beauty.

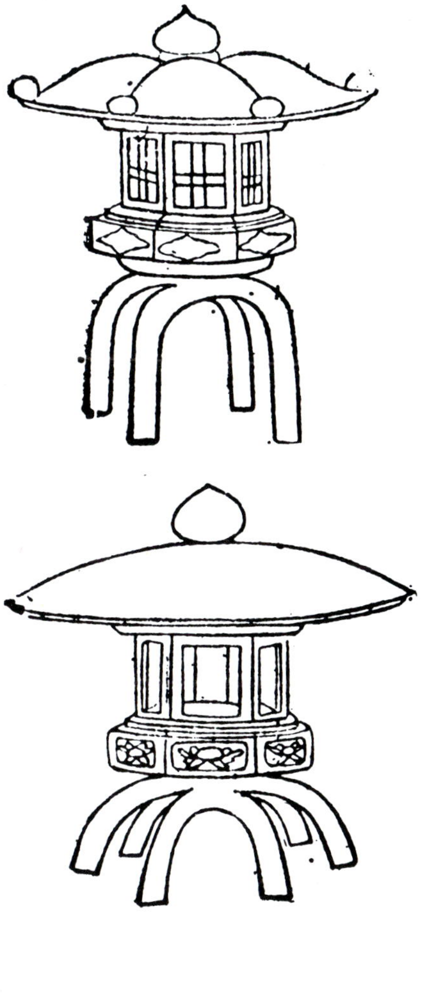

all the hustle and bustle of the world behind. The garden is usually divided into two parts, an inner and an outer part, and there should be a clear contrast between them. If the outer part of the garden is open to the sun, then the inner part should offer refreshing shade.

The central feature of the garden is

122 *A stone lantern; detail from the series* Thirty Views of Fuji *by Katsushika Hokusai (1833)*

123 *Two lanterns of the* yukimidoro *type, one with four and the other with six feet (woodcut)*

It was a practical consideration, in effect, which led the tea masters to enrich the composition of the garden path by adding *tobiishi* (literally flying stones). They are raised above the level of the path, and are at the right distance from each other to serve as a measure of one's steps. At the same time they protect the guest's snow-white socks from dew or raindrops where the path is brushed by tall grasses or ferns. The *tobiishi* technique quickly became very popular and is a permanent feature of private gardens today.

The practical aspect of this use of stone along the tea garden path did not detract from the natural beauty of the stone path, but increased it greatly. The path mirrors the gardener's talent for placing his chosen stones so that it is not only easy to walk along the path, but each single stone attracts the guest's eye by its shape and its harmonious relationship with its companions.

The choice of *tobiishi* stones, and their placing, was the outcome of long consideration, and the final decision was precise. There is a story of a *daimyo,* or baron, who asked Sen no Rikyu to arrange the stones on the path through his tea garden. The *daimyo* considered that the length of time the famous tea master thought over the positioning of each stone was exaggerated, so when the master left, the *daimyo* moved one of the stones a fraction feeling sure it would not be

125 *Making stone lanterns in the Middle Ages (woodcut)*

124 *Lanterns originally lit the approach to a temple. This is the temple of the Great Buddha, Kamakura*

noticed. The next day, however, as Rikyu looked at what he had done the previous day, he promptly moved the stone back to the position he had spent so long deciding upon in the first place.

The secret gardeners' handbooks set the height of the *tobiishi* according to where they are set along the path, and to their relationship with each other. The stones are divided into imperial, noble, actors' stones and ordinary people's stones, according to their height.

The *tobiishi* alternate with the carefully designed pattern of the paving stones; Kobori Enshu, in particular, made good use of the contrast between the natural forms of the *tobiishi* and the geometrical forms of the finished flagstones. Various methods were developed. One of particular interest was the 'scattered beans' method (*mamemaki ishi*). The translation suggests that stones are placed to look as if they had been thrown down at random, although in fact the

126 A tea garden of a private house with a yukimidoro lantern

127 A stone lantern, Toshogu, Nikko

design is very carefully worked out. Another favourite manner of paving used small pebbles of interesting shapes and colour; it was called 'barley-grain paving' (*arare jiki*).

The arrangement of stones on the path was also affected by such things as the age of the owner of the garden. The founder of the Uranosenke garden was already an old man when he had his tea garden laid out, and so the distance between the paving stones of the path fits the gait of an elderly person, taking short and careful steps.

The *tobiishi* are also a guide in matters of etiquette. In the Yabunouchi garden there is a stone on which the host comes to stand when welcoming his guests; the host then takes a step forward on to a slightly lower one in front when greeting the chief guest.

As each guest passes through the tea garden dressed in a kimono of subdued hue and wooden sandals, and approaches the tea house, the garden takes away his day-to-day worries, calms his mind and leads him towards deeper concentration. It is as though not seconds, but an age had passed as he moves a few steps on; as though past, present and future have merged into one continuous moving stream. The tea garden is a symbol of that movement and thus at the same time a symbol of human life itself.

As the guests pass from the outer garden to the inner garden through a rustic wooden gate, both physical and spiritual cleansing is provided for at the water basin. The moments spent by the basin represent more than the physical act of washing; they are moments of intense aesthetic experience. Whole books could be written about the care the tea masters spend on choosing their water basin, and on placing it in the garden.

The water basin itself is a combination of utility and elegance. The shapes are known as *chozubachi* or *tsukubai*, the latter denoting a vessel to which one must bend down. They vary not only according to the size of the garden and the taste of the owner, but also according to the different schools of the tea ceremony. In the earliest gardens, before the tea garden style evolved, the precursor of the water basin was probably a stone at the point where water flowed into the lake.

In the tea garden water is usually carried by a bamboo pipe, to fall into a vessel which appears weather worn on the outside but is scrupulously clean within. Sometimes it will be a stone from the seashore, hollowed by the waves; or a boulder from the foundations of a derelict temple; or the trough of a deserted well. It can be long like a kimono sleeve, or round with a hole in the centre like an old Japanese coin. In the Edo period new and more artful forms were introduced — cylindrical vessels, or vessels shaped like a pitcher, a boat, or Mount Fuji.

Practical considerations determined the height at which the water basin was placed, so that the guests would not have to bend too low. However, the Omotesenke school characteristically used a low round water basin with the opening slightly off centre; it was placed in a dry stream bed among ferns and grasses. This type of basin was very fitting for tea gardens of the hermitage type, as were those formed by hollowing out a fallen tree trunk, or using other natural materials. Kobori Enshu, on the other hand, preferred water basins of dressed stone. His square basin is well-known. By this example he illustrated that just as water takes the shape of the vessel which holds it, so people adapt themselves to their friends and surroundings.

Each stone placed by the basin has a practical use and is positioned to create a harmony. The stone to the right of the basin was called *yutoishi,* and on chilly days a vessel of warm water was placed there. To the left was the stone to hold a candle. This was the basic composition, which the master of the tea ceremony or the owner of the garden would develop according to his own tastes.
In winter the water basin was filled with sand, to prevent damage, and sometimes a little roof was placed over it in autumn, to protect it from falling leaves.

Even the shape of the hole through which water was poured after use was the subject of aesthetic consideration to maintain the harmony of this part of the garden where scrupulous cleanliness was always observed.

Not far from the water basin there stood a stone lantern. These lanterns came to Japan along with Buddhist temple architecture, and were also used in Shinto temples. From the end of the 16th century they became an essential feature of the tea gardens, where they served an important practical purpose. At first they were used mainly to light the garden during the nocturnal tea ceremony known as 'night conversation', which lasted from evening until dawn. Later they were always lit as evening fell, to guide thc guests through the garden. The light of the lamp was also the symbol of the light of knowledge, driving away the 'shadows of ignorance'.

The old gardeners' handbooks

128 Stone lanterns, Nara

stressed that on a dark night the lantern should shed enough light to prevent the guests from stumbling, while on a moonlit night it should not shine too brightly. The lamplight should not dispel the darkness, but emphasize its charms, still allowing the night to remain night.

There were five main parts to the stone lantern: the shade (*kasa*), the flame bed (*hibukuro*), the central section (*chudai*), the stem (*sao*) and the base (*gedai*). This basic scheme was developed by Japanese masters of the tea ceremony and stone carvers into innumerable forms. The decoration of the lanterns was often derived from Buddhist symbolism. The lotus was a favourite motif, the petals ornamenting the base and central section while the upper part was carved in the shape of a lotus flower.

Oribe's lanterns are sometimes thought to show a Christian influence, because their simple lines bear a faint resemblance to the cross. These date from the time when Christians were persecuted in Japan.

Lanterns were named after the Buddhist temples from whence they came, or after famous masters of the tea ceremony like Sen no Rikyu, Furuta Oribe, Kobori Enshu and others. It was not unusual for a lantern to have its own life story. The names sometimes referred to the seasons, like the *yukimidoro* lantern (literally, looking at the snow); presumably so named because it looked most beautiful when there was a powdering of snow on the lamp-shade.

The low three-section lanterns had symbolic significance: the upper part represented heaven, the central part with the flame, man and the base, the earth. The five-section lantern symbolized the five elements from which everything in life derives, the *go-rin*.

The making of lanterns is still a well-known and highly appreciated craft in Japan, although they now adorn the modern residential gardens as well as the tea gardens. When the guest has ceremonially rinsed his mouth with water from the long-handled wooden scoop, the first phase of preparation for the tea ceremony is complete. He stands by the water basin relaxed and able to concentrate on the beauty of the things around him, feeling as if he had travelled a long way from his normal world. In fact, the garden acts as a kind of an 'overture' to the tea ceremony.

To carry this analogy further, the creators of tea gardens are like composers of music. They know how to slow down the rhythm of the guest's steps along the path, so that he can appreciate the bent lines of a pine branch, or lift his eyes to the crown of a maple glowing in its autumn tints. The Japanese derive particular pleasure from the soft carpet of moss whose velvety green forms an essential element of a garden.

129 A stone lantern, Horyuji

130 Lanterns for tea gardens were often designed by masters of the tea ceremony. The carved Oribe lantern (left) was designed by Furuta Oribe and the Enshu lantern (right) by Kobori Enshu (17th-century woodcut)

131 *Temple gardens were originally illuminated by wooden lanterns*

For Sen no Rikyu thick moss, clean and drenched in sunlight, was an integral part of the tea garden, together with a moonlit night and dew-spangled summer dawn. He found in moss, in particular, the realization of all the qualities of *wabi,* the aesthetic principle which is the soul of the tea ceremony.

Thick low bushes in the tea garden suggested forests. Later, influenced by various trends in landscape gardening, low continuous trimmed hedges were introduced along the path, as well as hedges clipped into various shapes, especially close to the gate. It still remained the custom not to plant deciduous trees, with the exception of the plum, in front of the gate.

The general effect of the colours in the garden round the tea house is subdued. Few flowers were planted to offer any contrast to the dark green of the trees and the bushes. This restraint gave all the greater prominence to the beauty of the flower arrangement inside the tea house.

This point is well illustrated by the story of Hideyoshi, the 16th-century military ruler of Japan, who once expressed the desire to see convolvulus growing in the garden of the master, Sen no Rikyu. He was known to have grown the flower from seed especially brought from abroad. The elderly master of the tea ceremony invited Hideyoshi to take tea with him early in the morning, when the blooms of the morning glory open and the stem is crowded with blossom. Imagine Hideyoshi's surprise, however, when he entered the garden and saw not a single morning glory. The spot where they had been growing was bare, covered over with sand and fine gravel. Only when he entered the tea house did he see a single white morning glory gleaming in an antique bronze vase placed in the recess; the petals still damp with the morning dew.

This story gives us the key to an understanding of the Japanese conception of beauty as a profound aesthetic experience. A similar story is told of Iehara Jizen, the owner of a famous bamboo vase. When he wanted to show the vase to a valued friend during the New Year tea ceremony, he built a new tea house in which not a single piece of bamboo was used, and even dug up the bamboos growing in the garden.

It is time to move further along the path from the water basin where the guest sees that part of the garden which suggests the tea house itself is near. The walls can be seen through the foliage, and the low doorway comes into sight. The guests wait on a wooden seat (*koshikake*) protected by a roof, until their host comes to welcome them with a bow. In the past guests would also retire to this bench during a break (*nakaji*) in the tea ceremony.

From this bench *tobiishi* lead to the corner of the garden devoted to the needs of hygiene. This is yet more proof that there is nothing so prosaic in life that it cannot be treated aesthetically and at the same time symbolize the ephemeral nature of the material world and the place of human life in the eternal round of nature. Guests usually admire this area with its two flat stones surrounded by scrupulously clean, gleaming white sand.

132 Moss and stone in harmony in a tea garden

Also near the tea house lies a pit for garden refuse, skilfully hidden behind bushes or a wicker or bamboo fence. This is so designed as to not only hide an unpleasant sight, but to provide a setting for a stone lamp, or an azalea or other shrub.

From outside, the tea house is unprepossessing, resembling nothing more than a poor peasant hut with a very low front entrance. Stones lead from the waiting bench to the *noriishi*, the last stone, on which one steps up to the entrance. According to ancient custom there is a two-level stone or a shelf beside the door. Here swords were laid aside, for in the Middle Ages not even nobles and samurai were allowed to bear arms within the tea house, although they were never parted from their two swords anywhere else. In the tea house social distinctions between nobles and bourgeois disappeared; at least for a while.

A broom hangs on the wall of the tea house, but even this humble object has an aura of timelessness in this Japanese setting. The task of sweeping the garden early in the morning or in the mild evening air had a most calming effect and was one of the favourite duties of tea masters.

Cleanliness is an essential part of both the tea garden and of the tea ceremony itself, but sweeping is a subtle operation performed with a light touch rather than a drastic application of hygiene. Sen no Rikyu is said to have set his son to sweep the garden in readiness for guests. When the boy had finished, Rikyu went to inspect the garden, but he was not satisfied. The boy set to work again, but again his father was unable to praise him. And so he knelt before his father, bowed low, and asked: 'What more can I do, father? I have swept the path and raked up the leaves. The moss is bright green and there is not

133 *A lantern in a tea garden. The edges of the pond have been planted with ornamental grasses*

134 *A composition of stones, evergreen shrubs and conifers*

a scrap of dirt anywhere.'

'You still do not understand, my son,' answered Rikyu, and going into the garden he shook the maple tree until its beautiful crimson leaves lay scattered everywhere.

Before entering the tea house the guests take off their sandals, and kneel to enter by the low door, emphasizing the humility and the equality of all those taking part in the ceremony. Sometimes the guests have a spare pair of socks with them to change into as they sit on the waiting bench, in case a tiny speck of dirt has clung to the pair they were wearing.

The room where the ceremony takes place is small and very simple. The host's individual taste is revealed in the choice of the scroll painting on the wall, the way the flowers are arranged in the vase in the *tokonoma* recess, the choice of bowls for tea drinking and the other utensils, and the way the open hearth is arranged in the middle of the floor.

135 A garden in gyo *style with artificial hills (woodcut)*

136 A modern tea pavilion set by a lake

The arrangement of flowers for the tea ceremony is a special form of *ikebana*. Simplicity is the keynote, and often the vase holds no more than a single bloom, or a carefully selected branch which accords with the mood of the day.

The scroll painting is most often a calligraphic quotation from one of the Zen philosophers on the subject of calmness, illumination, or the unity of man with nature. For this type of calligraphy a natural flowing line of the brush strokes is characteristic, expressing peace of mind.

The white ricepaper covering the windows of the tea house lets in a subdued light and enables the host to regulate the lighting of the room according to the time of day. It appears from the descriptions of tea ceremonies staged by the great masters that there was a special charm about gathering early in the morning while the dew was still fresh on the ground; on a moonlit evening; or during the late afternoon in winter time, when the garden was lightly covered with snow. Nevertheless the most frequently chosen time for the tea ceremony was the early afternoon.

On entering the room, the guests find themselves alone for a while to give them time to get used to their surroundings and to appreciate the good taste of their host. When he eventually joins them from a small adjacent room, he greets them once more with a low bow, and exchanges a few words with the principal guest, usually on the subject of the scroll painting or the *ikebana*. The time has then come when the guests can enjoy their host's ability to create an atmosphere of *wabi* by his ingenious choice of utensils, while they drink their bowl of tea. The utensils are simple but at the same time of a refined

137 A tea house

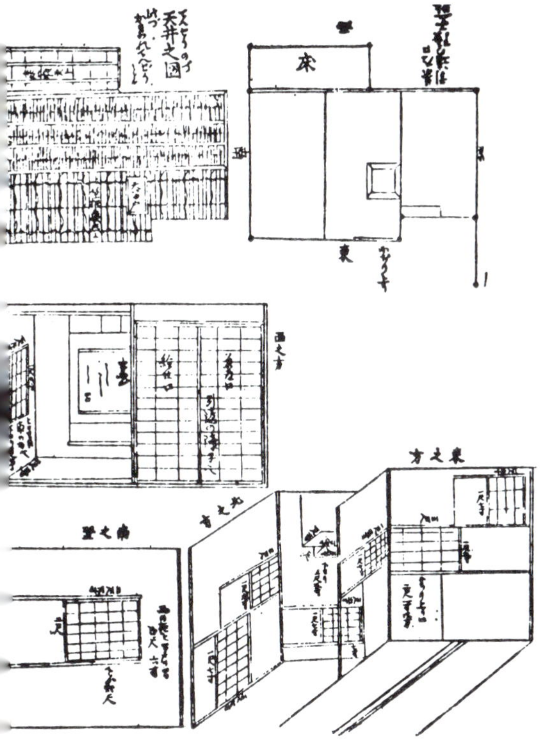

138 A tea house divided in the traditional manner by sliding partitions

elegance. The decoration on them often reflects the season of the year. In summer they may suggest a cooling breeze; in winter warmth and comfort. A source of special delight is the sound of water bubbling in the iron kettle over the charcoal fire. Over three hundred years ago the master Takuan wrote in his diary: 'The host greeted his guests and they all listened in silence to the water bubbling in the kettle. The sound recalled the wind blowing through the pine branches by the seashore. It was a moment in which they forgot all their sorrows and tribulations . . .'

'Nothing should be allowed to

139 *Detail of a landscape (probably 16th century) by the Chinese painter Ch'iou Ying. This is an example of the type of painting that greatly influenced Japanese artists and garden designers*

140 *Kano Hideyori:* Looking at the maples, *a 16th-century painting on a screen. This depicts one of the festive occasions for drinking tea*

disturb this moment,' wrote Sen no Rikyu, 'especially no talk of religion, the neighbours' property, relatives, wars or human passions and vices.' This became the general rule among his followers.

At the time when the tea ceremony came into being all the work in noble and bourgeois households was done by servants, so the physical act of preparing tea and all that went with it became a symbol of the host's humility towards his guests.

During the ceremony the host takes a bamboo spoon of tea powder from the pottery or lacquer tea-caddy, and puts two or three spoonsful into a wide pottery bowl. He pours a scoop of boiling water on to the tea and beats it to a froth with a bamboo whisk. The bowl is then presented to the principal guest, who takes a sip and passes the bowl to the next person. The most important aspect is the grace with which both the host and the guests perform these prescribed gestures. (Nowadays each guest is given a separate bowl.)

141 *A garden lantern placed close to a low water basin (woodcut)*

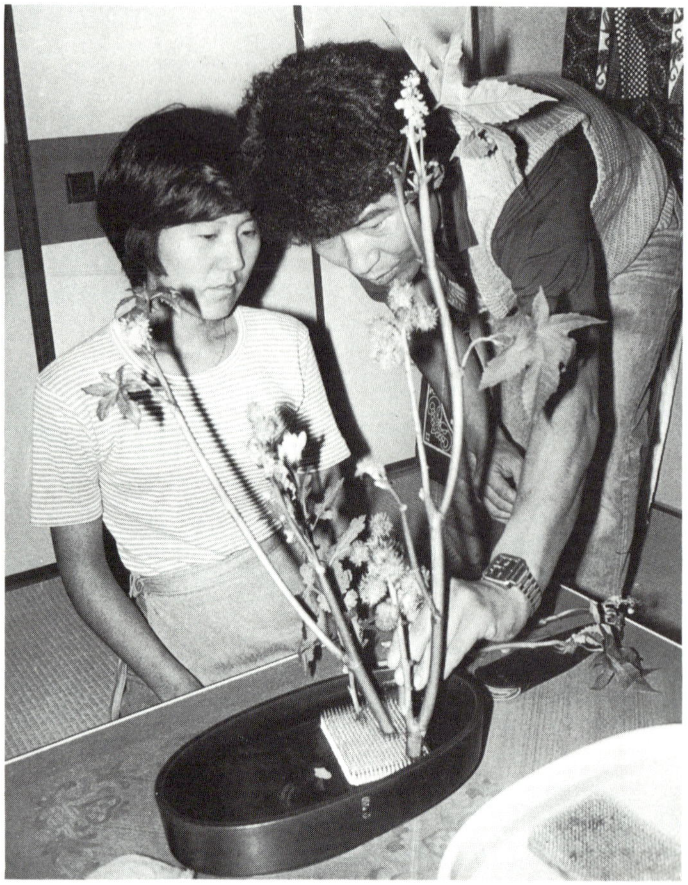

142 Ikebana *is an essential feature of the room where tea is drunk, and is an aesthetic part of the tea ceremony*

The tea is bitter – that, too, is an element of *wabi.* The bitter taste is sometimes emphasized by handing round one or two sweetmeats at the beginning of the ceremony. In earlier times a light, simple dish called *kaiseki* was served. This expression is derived from the days when Zen monks used to carry a warm stone on their chest to drive away the pangs of hunger.

Everything used during the tea ceremony is marked by its simplicity. The instructions drawn up by the tea masters inspired and indeed still do inspire Japanese artists and craftsmen to create new and original designs for spoons, lacquer trays and tea caddies, baskets to hold flowers and many other little articles.

The tea ceremony has contributed much to the cultivated elegance of Japanese behaviour. The walk through the garden calms and relaxes the guests so that once inside the small space of the tea house all those present behave with courtesy and grace. The host must spend a long time and display a great deal of patience and perseverance before he attains mastery in his role (from the moment he greets his guests in the garden to the final farewell at the gate). The ceremonial drinking of tea in the tea house and the surrounding garden creates a suitable atmosphere for discussion of aesthetic and philosophical subjects, according to the

143 *Plant motifs decorate traditional pottery from Karatsu used in the tea ceremony*

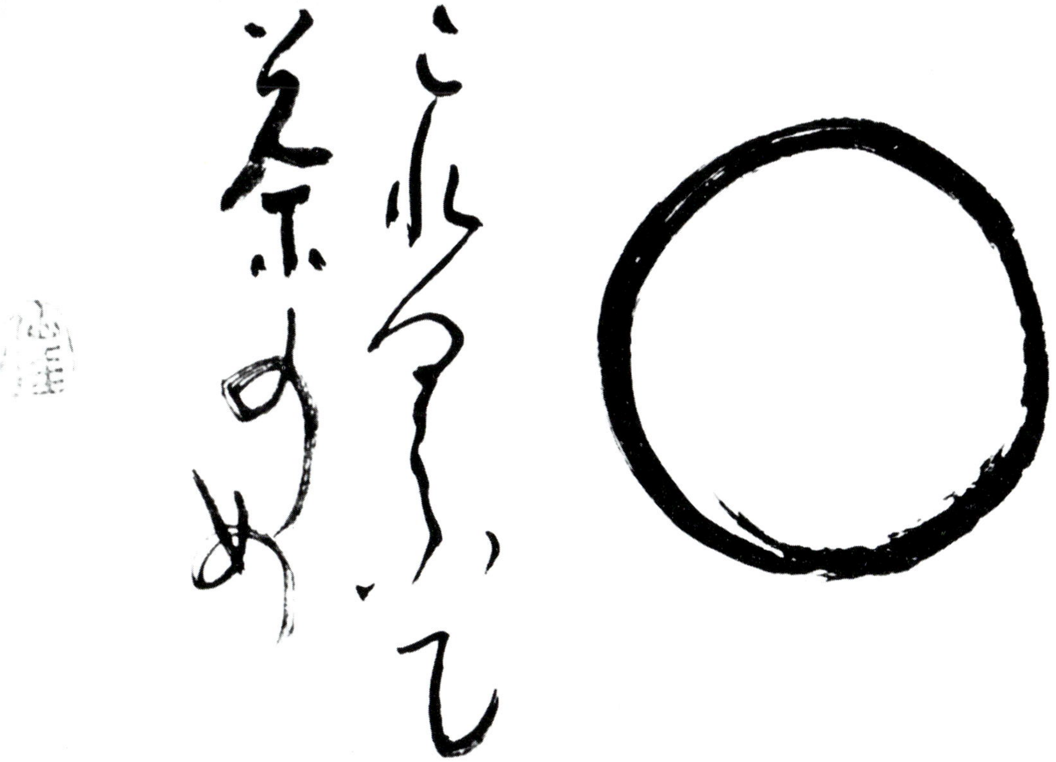

144 *Sengai:* A circle, *a painting in the Zen style. Pictures of this kind were hung in the tea house*

abilities of those present. Nature and the garden the guests have passed through are one of the first topics of conversation.

Naturally, with the enormous popularity of the tea ceremony at all levels of society, the conversation is often confined to conventional expressions of admiration for the tea utensils, the *ikebana,* the scroll painting, the arrangement of the room and the principal or most striking features of the garden.

Details of the ceremony vary according to different masters and different schools of thought but, generally speaking, after spending about two hours in the house the special mood that has been so carefully created gradually fades and the guests return through the tea garden. However, the transition back to reality should not be sudden, and the guests should still be able to enjoy their experience long after the ceremony has come to an end.

'The tea ceremony would lose its meaning if those who take part cannot find pleasure in the gleaming white snow and the refreshing rain,' the old masters used to say. They believed that on such days the spiritual mood of the guests could be recognized from the tap of their wooden sandals on the stones of the path. In winter, gardeners often spread pine needles over the moss to protect it, and wrap delicate trees and bushes in straw.

145 The tea ceremony

In the course of the history of the tea ceremony the leaders of the principal schools laid out large gardens with several tea houses each surrounded by their own small garden. This led to a flourishing art in designing hedges and gates (mostly of a rustic type with a thatched roof over them) which in time became an accepted craft. This is reflected in the design of private gardens. One particularly interesting feature was the bamboo wall (*agesunoko*). These were used where one tea garden passed into another.

Furuta Oribe, Kobori Enshu and Honami Koetsu[57)] introduced novel elements into the design of the tea garden, freeing it from the restraints of nature. They dared to use straight lines and geometrical forms which had been hitherto unthinkable. This was particularly apparent in patterns of paving stones and in the shapes of lamps and water basins. They laid greater stress on aesthetic effect than on utility. In their new conception the tea garden followed the principle of *sakiagari*: trees became higher the further away they were from the tea house, while in Rikyu's conception it was the reverse — there was a tall tree by the tea house and the plants decreased slightly in height towards the garden boundaries.

Sometimes the tea ceremony was held in the garden itself. In some of the great gardens, like the Hamarikyu garden in Tokyo, meetings are still arranged on great occasions, when the masters of different schools come together along with their disciples.

There can be no doubt that the tea ceremony is still a very important institution in Japan. In the restless atmosphere of big city life it is a peaceful refuge, still greatly valued and sought after. As long as the ceremony exists, the art of the tea garden will continue to develop.

146 *Today, the tea ceremony is known as* nodate *when it is held outside in the garden*

147 *Clipped bushes by a door, Daitokuji, Kyoto*

148 *The entrance to the imperial garden Shugakuin, Kyoto*

To those who are waiting for the flowers to bloom, I would love to show this gleaming patch of green in the midst of a snow-covered village . . .

Fujiwara no Ietaka

Gardens of the Edo period

It was a characteristic feature of the evolution of the Japanese garden that gradually different styles developed according to the function ascribed to the garden, and that the aesthetic conceptions which guided their designs developed under strong religious and philosophical influences.

At the end of the 16th century, when Japan was again united after a

149 *Fencing inside the great garden, Nijo, Kyoto*

150 *The bamboo gate leading to the tea house in the imperial garden Shugakuin, Kyoto*

period of unrest and was approaching the zenith of its medieval culture, the social changes which ensued were also reflected in garden design. They did not, however, involve a break with centuries' old traditions. On the contrary, the old traditions were revived and given new opportunities in the large encircling gardens known as *kaiyushiki*.

These gardens were a synthesis of the existing styles and served a similar function to the parks which surrounded the country seats of the European aristocracy. Since they formed part of the specifically Japanese way of life, their composition was different and so was their inner meaning. In many respects, to go back to a musical analogy, they resembled a symphony. For like this musical form they were composed of a central idea threading through the

151 *A path of square flagstones and steps lead up to a bridge, Katsura, Kyoto*

152 *Path with steps, Rinnoji, Nikko*

entire work which linked a number of motifs and variations.

The composition of these complex gardens made considerable demands on the designer. It was their purpose to encourage a more profound appreciation of nature by directing the eye to the varied scenery and to different aspects of the garden, thus creating a run up to the final dramatic experience.

Among the famous gardens which were designed in this style are Samboin, Katsura, Shugakuin, Santogosho and the other great gardens of Kyoto, Ritsurin in Takamatsu, Korakuen in Tokyo and Okoyama, and many others scattered throughout Japan[59].

The central element in the composition of the *kaiyushiki* gardens was a large lake. This was a link with the traditions of the Heian gardens, not least because it was frequently intended for boating, so that the beauties of the surrounding landscape could be appreciated from the water. The symbolism of the islands of the legend of Horai persisted, too, although usually only as mere

153 *Aerial view of the path through the Shiba garden, Tokyo*

suggestions. The scenery was made more interesting by the construction of artificial hills.

The *kaiyushiki* gardens included such existing features as the tea garden and, to provide a complete contrast, the dry garden. The surrounding landscape was used, particularly thoughtfully, to bring out the full value of the composition of the garden itself. There were other interesting features incorporated in it; such as the re-creation of famous beauty spots; a custom which also goes back to the Heian period.

The central focus of the garden was the mansion, usually in *shoin* style. It was designed to be in harmony with the surrounding scenery and with the architecture of the tea houses, pavilions and summerhouses. All these structures are essential elements of the composition and help to create the order which governs it; the path provides the link between the different parts of the garden, winding and changing direction according to the designer's demands. The path increases the impact of the scenery by leading the visitor to interesting viewpoints of the garden — a pause for rest by a stone lantern, water basin by a waterfall or tea house, or in the dry garden, offer the occasion for surprise and enjoyment.

The path itself was one of the outstanding creations of the designer of the garden. It served a practical purpose without departing from the overall aesthetic conception of the garden. As a rule it attracted attention by the ingenuity with which stones of varying sizes and shapes were combined in patterns which today serve as models for modern architecture. The style of the paving also reflects the two main trends in garden design that emerged during the course of the 17th century. These were the style of straight lines and geometrical forms, introduced by Furuta Oribe and Kobori Enshu, and the conservative style in which nature was manipulated in such a way as to leave as little sign of human intervention as was possible, however great it might be in reality.

It was characteristic of the garden path that continuous paving alternated with irregularly placed stones, such as have been described in the previous chapter devoted to tea gardens. Parts of the path, which were in constant use, were paved all over with small stones to ensure a comfortable passage in all weathers. The path leading from the gate to the house was treated in this way. Where the visitor should be alone with his thoughts, however, his steps were slowed down by irregularly placed *tobiishi* chosen for their beauty. They were arranged so as to direct his gaze towards a point of interest such as a nearby waterfall or a lantern hidden among the bushes, to draw his eyes upwards to the mountains beyond the garden, or downwards to the lake. The stones used where two paths crossed were large and flat, allowing the visitor time to consider which way to take. Where the garden took on a more open character, the path became easy, surfaced with sand or fine gravel.

The stones most frequently used for paving were marl, flint or granite. The histories of gardens and the diaries of master gardeners often give the place from which stone was brought for use in the garden. It is known that when Kobori Enshu was laying out the Sentogisho garden in Kyoto[59] he ordered a large number of boulders from as far away as Odawara, several hundred kilometres to the north. The care with which the stones were moved can be judged by the fact that every single rock was wrapped in cotton cloth.

Where the path comes up to the water's edge the artfulness and the imagination of the gardener came into their own. There were two main ways of treating this problem, either

154 Stepping stones resembling bridge piers are a much admired feature in a path round a garden

155 Stream bed paved with stones is spanned by a bridge formed by a single stone

by means of a ford or a bridge. To make a ford stones were placed with their upper surface above the water, so as to make the most of the part of the stone which was submerged, especially when it was of a particularly beautiful shape or colour. The best-known ford of this type is that in the Suizenji garden in Kumamotu, on the island of Kyushu. Sometimes the ford is composed of stones shaped

157 The original layout of the garden round the castle of Himeji

158 Clipped bushes in the inner castle garden, Himeji ▶

156 The castle of Himeji. Large landscape gardens originally surrounded the castles and the summer palaces of the aristocracy

like bridge piers and placed chequer-board fashion in the water.

When the path to the water is merely a branch off the main path to reach the lake or brook, then it ends at the water's edge or continues symbolically under the water. The stones can be seen clearly through the transparent water, and look refreshing to the visitor in the summer heat.

Bridges are an important factor in the artistic treatment of different parts of the garden where their position determines both their shape and the choice of material. Some of the bridges are purely symbolical and help to complete the atmosphere of a certain part of the garden, but most of them are used and walked over. They cross streams, link islands with the mainland or take the visitor across inlets in the lake. In gardens where the lake is deep enough to allow boating, a steep 'drum' bridge has its practical advantages, for the boats can pass beneath it, as in the Samboin garden in Kyoto. These bridges are made of logs with a surface of beaten clay.

The *yatsubashi* type of bridge is well known and is formed by eight planks laid chequer-board fashion on low piers. It inspired Ogate Korin[60] in his design for a lacquer writing box. Later the same motif fascinated the Impressionists and Art Nouveau painters in Europe.

The steep bridges give a fine view over the garden; the most famous was the red lacquer bridge in the garden of the Katsura villa, but it has unfortunately not survived. The 'half moon' bridge in the Ritsurin garden in Takamatsu[61], one of the most extensive gardens in Japan, is particularly steep, and offers a magnificent view of the surroundings.

Some bridges are roofed over, like

the Chitose bridge in the Shugakuin-rikyu. In the Hama garden, now hemmed in by densely populated Tokyo, the gardeners designed three bridges each with a pergola supporting flowering wisteria. Where the atmosphere was one of wooded retreat, simple bridges constructed of large flagstones remained popular.

Compositions in stone were not of such importance in the *kaiyushiki* gardens as they had been in earlier styles. However, an exception can be found in one of the earliest *kaiyushiki*

159 *Pergola with wisteria. Garden of the Imperial Palace, Kyoto*

160 *A woodcut by Hishikawa Moronobu:* Garden Pastimes, *listening to bird-song by the garden aviary*

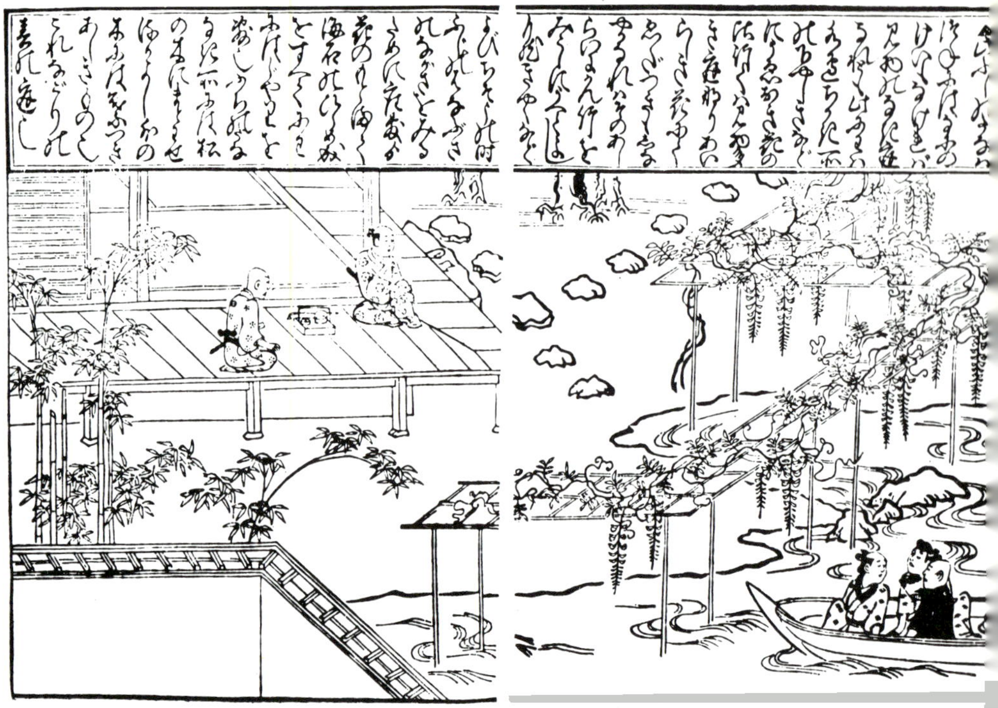

161 *A woodcut by Hishikawa Moronobu:* Garden Pastimes, *looking at the wisteria from a boat*

162 *An important element in the large* kaiyu *gardens was to have bridges placed correctly. The Onrindo chapel, Katsura, Kyoto*

gardens, that of Samboin, which was re-laid at the end of the 16th century. The military ruler of Japan at that time, Hideyoshi Toyotomi, gathered an enormous number of rocks there, and even today there are over seven hundred remaining. They include Hideyoshi's favourite stone, the Fuji-toishi, whose story is so exciting that it has been recorded by Japanese chroniclers. The ex-emperor Gomizunoo[62] is also known to have made clay models of the stones he wanted for his garden at Shugakuin, so that his gardeners could then search out the correct shaped stones. The garden in the Nijo palace in Kyoto[63], laid out by Kobori Enshu in 1624, is also known as *Hachijin no niwa* (the garden of eight military camps) as groups of stones have been arranged

166 Steep stone bridge at the Hachimangu shrine, Kamakura

◀ 163 A woodcut by Hishikawa Moronobu: Garden Pastimes, *the flower festival*

◀ 164 'Drum' bridge with a pine bending low over the water

165 Lacquer tray decorated with a garden bridge

to represent military camps.

In the Edo period less and less attention was paid to the use of stones, for gardens were becoming more lyrical, more feminine in their charm, and acquiring a different character from those of the past. Towards the end of the Edo period, in the early 19th century, low rounded stones were most in demand.

Together with this general change in the character of the *kaiyushiki* garden in the Edo period, slow-moving streams and brooks gained great popularity. The garden became open to the light, the scene for quiet walks and leisure, and the setting for social occasions such as admiring the spring flowers, the autumn tints, or the reflection of moonlight upon the water. At points where these attractions were particularly spectacular pavilions and summer-houses were built with such poetic names as *Rakushiken* (cottage of joy), *Riuntei* (pavilion that touches the clouds) or *Shokatei* (pavilion of delight in flowers).

For the most part the tea houses

built in these large aristocratic gardens were no longer in the rustic *soan* style, but in the sober *shoin* style. This did not mean, that there might not be both types in the same garden. Visitors would stop to look into the tea house as they walked in the garden, but the tea ceremony was held there only on special occasions.

Stone lanterns added variety to the *kaiyushiki* with their varied shapes, their interesting stories and attractive names. Together with the water basin they gave the final touch to a composition and emphasized the charm of waterfalls and lakes. New and original designs were created; tall lanterns were usually made with a single base, while low ones stood on four or even six feet. Lanterns on two feet were

167 The Mihashi bridge, Nikko

particularly admired, and so were those designed to hang out over the water.

Hotaru-doro lanterns were very well-known, and their light dancing on the water at night was reminiscent of a swarm of fireflies. The *sodegata-doro,* or sleeve lamp, was a very strange form based on a kimono sleeve. Kobori Enshu introduced shapes which seem almost cubist in their design, judging from his 'three light' lantern (*sanko-doro*), shaped like a block of stone with three openings through which the light shone. This lantern looks as though it has been made by the hands of a 20th-century sculptor, rather than those of a master so many centuries ago. Of the other types of lantern we should mention the *yagura-doro* (spired lantern), the *yamadera-doro* (temple lantern), the *takimi-doro* (waterfall lantern) and *Chosen-doro* (Korean lantern).

Just as the lanterns retained their popularity in the *kaiyushiki,* so did the water basins for washing the hands and rinsing the mouth, which also came from the tea garden. Another influence of Chinese painting produced a fashion for miniature pagodas in these large aristocratic gardens.

The clipping of trees and bushes acquired great importance in all types of garden during the Edo period, including the *kaiyushiki.* Careful study of landscape paintings and of nature itself led the gardeners to make constant improvements in their techniques. Besides the 'great shaping', which was applied to tall trees, the shaping of evergreen bushes –

168 Detail of the Mihashi bridge, Nikko

169 A bridge in the inner garden of the Imperial Palace, Kyoto

'low shaping', as it was called, became very popular. The bushes were trimmed to represent stones, waves or waterfalls. It was not the gardeners' aim to force an unnatural symmetry on the garden, but to stress by bold cutting the natural lines of the scenery.

Large gardens, often many hectares in extent, were laid out in places where the traditional gardeners' technique of *shakei* or 'borrowed scenery' could be used. The city of Kyoto was ideal for this type of landscape garden, with its mountainous scenery on three sides. The gardens merge into the great wooded expanse on the hillsides, as at Nikko[64], or harmonize with the seashore as at Miyajima, where the designer made use of the changing effects caused by the tides[65].

170 Part of the Futoarasan shrine, Nikko

It became a great fashion in the aristocratic gardens of the 18th century to reproduce famous beauty spots from all over Japan. This was in some measure due to the policy of the Tokugawa shoguns, who in order to contain the power of the great provincial barons ordered them to make regular journeys to Edo, the seat of the military government of the land, and to spend a certain amount of time there. The barons then took pleasure in recreating in their gardens the beauty spots they had passed through on their travels. Miniature Mount Fuji began to appear, together with replicas of some of the fifty-three stopping places found along the Tokaido road linking Edo with the imperial capital of Kyoto. The owner of the Rikugien garden in Edo had several dozen of such famous beauty spots on the Wakanoura coast, not far from Wakayama, reproduced in his estates. The use of Chinese names gave an exotic air to some gardens, like the Ritsurin garden in Takamatsu, where the six lakes were named after the best known lakes in China, and the thirteen hills were named after mountains famous in Chinese history.

It was also the custom to invite poets to choose the most beautiful spot in the garden; Reizan Tamemura chose the 'ten landscapes of celestial beauty' in the Sentogosho garden.

Different sounds formed part of the

171 The entrance to the main building, Nijo Palace, Kyoto

172 Kamoidera temple at Hamamatsu. Plan for a large landscape garden (woodcut)

173 Part of the inner garden of the Imperial Palace, Kyoto

174 Wooden lanterns at the entrance to a small Shinto shrine

impression given by a garden, be it of water, a breeze or even of insects. The murmur of a waterfall should be heard by visitors from afar, even if it was a long way removed from the thunderous roar of the 90 metre (300 foot) high Nikko waterfall, which served as a model for so many gardeners.

A babbling brook, the sound of water dropping from a bamboo pipe into a stone basin, rain falling in spring or autumn; all helped to enhance the poetic atmosphere. One of the emperors had a shingle roof added to his palace, so that he could enjoy the sound of the rain falling. For the same reason broad-leaved trees, bushes and flowers were planted near the house. The visitor's attentive ear would not miss the quiet splash of a fish coming up for air or

175 *Large gardens were laid out round Shinto and Buddhist shrines, Futoarasan, Nikko*

176 *A* torii *gate and garden lanterns mark the presence of a spring*

the soft step of the deer in the undergrowth.

Games and sports also had their special place in the garden — archery, falconry, riding and a kind of football known as *kemari.* It is not surprising to learn from their diaries that one of the duties of the gardener was to wash pine trees left dusty by such pastimes.

According to the suitability of the terrain of the garden, there were other sports and pastimes to be enjoyed. In the Shibarikyu garden of Edo there was fishing; in the Happo-en garden wild ducks were caught in long-handled nets, a custom which is still carried on in some of the imperial gardens.

The lightness of touch, the poetic mood and the leisurely lifestyle for which the *kaiyushiki* were designed

177 Low clipped bushes representing stones

179 *A shrub clipped to resemble the adjacent rock in the Nijo garden, Kyoto*

178 *Different ways of clipping trees; the* hako-zukuri, *box trimming style, predominates (woodcut)*

180 *Clipped shrubs in the Nijo garden, Kyoto*

182 The Kegon waterfall, Nikko, was often copied in landscape gardens

181 The Nachi waterfall, by an unknown painter probably of the 13th century. This painting was admired for centuries by landscape gardeners, and served as the model for their waterfalls

183 A garden waterfall set in a landscape typical of that found in Tokaido. A design for landscape gardeners (woodcut)

184 The tea pavilion in the Ritsurin garden, Takamatsu. Ritsurin is one of the largest and loveliest gardens in Japan

have much in common with the ancient Heian gardens, although their usage was much more varied. The *kaiyushiki* gardens with the carefully balanced treatment of their terrain and their intricate composition, are dependent on the high degree of technical skill of their creators. It is in these gardens that one may apply the term landscape gardening in the modern sense of the words. Many of these *kaiyushiki* gardens have now become parks open to the public.

The garden of the Katsura Villa in Kyoto[66] holds a special place among *kaiyushiki* gardens. It was one of the first as well as one of the finest examples of this style. Although it dates from the Middle Ages, it still serves as a model for a perfect environment for living. There is no break between the garden and the architecture of the house; they merge into each other, complementing each other perfectly. All the old traditions are here, presented in a new and attractive guise. Katsura is an unforgettable experience for every non-Japanese visitor; every detail opens a new vision of the world. To understand the significance of what is seen brings home to the visitor the realization of how life can be enriched if only people are capable of appreciating the beauty of simple things. It is in this sense that Katsura has made a great contribution to world civilization.

Katsura rikyu was built, like many other gardens, for the Prince Toshihito[68], on the site of a famous Heian garden, in a lovely part of the country with abundant water from the nearby river. The first part of the house to be built was The Old Shoin, originally the prince's town house but moved to Katsura in 1620–24. Toshihito's son, Prince Noritada, carried on with his father's plans and built two more parts onto the house, The Middle and The New Shoin. This was in preparation for a visit from the emperor Gomizunoo, who was a connoisseur and lover of gardens. (One of his claims to fame was for laying out the garden of Shugakuin.)

For a long time it was not at all certain who had really been responsible for designing Katsura; it is traditionally attributed to Kobori Enshu, but recent research has thrown doubt on this. It is now certain that Prince Toshihito conceived the garden himself, incorporating his own views on

185 *Tea pavilion by the lake, Ritsurin, Takamatsu*

186 *Garden bridges, Myoshinji, Kyoto (woodcut)*

187 A bridge in the Ritsurin garden, Takamatsu

life into the design. He was an educated nobleman who lived at a time when the country was ruled by the Tokugawa shoguns; the emperor and his court were condemned to a quiet but powerless existence in Kyoto while the real centre of authority moved to Edo.

It is known that Toshihito was a connoisseur of old Japanese literature and that he had a longing to revive the traditions of the Heian imperial court, at least in the environment of his summer residence. Japanese scholars believe that certain parts of the garden were direct interpretations of scenes from Heian poetry and prose. Katsura derives its inner dynamism, however, from the interaction of the lyricism of the old traditions and the remarkably uncompromising freedom of line introduced into Japanese gardens by Furuta Oribe and Kobori Enshu, and most clearly applied in the treatment of the paving of the main path.

Katsura spreads over an area of six and a quarter square kilometres (two

188 Villa Katsura, Kyoto

and half square miles) along the western bank of the river of the same name, and is enveloped in greenery. The path to the garden passes through several gates; besides the general purpose gate there is the ceremonial *Onarigomon* gate with the Imperial Gate beyond. The Middle Gate is further on still and is approached by the famous 'Chinese path' (*miyukimichi*), paved with small stones to its full width. This was the path the imperial processions took to reach the house; the Emperor's palanquin could be borne right into the mossy courtyard with its little hill and stone lantern, close to the house.

The house itself is of such simple design that it looks as though it had been designed by a 20th-century architect. The lines are straight and the proportions are determined by multiples of the length and breadth of *tatami* mats, giving a harmonious order to the whole design. The principal decorative components of the house are the dark brown beams and the white sliding doors of ricepaper. With only a few movements of the hand, the rooms of the house are open to the garden on two sides. The framework of the walls becomes filled with a view of the garden which changes as the visitor moves from room to room; the house literally merges into the garden.

The overhanging roofs of the low *shoin* rest on wooden columns, and the elegant line of the roof carries on towards the ground in the *amaochimizo* which carry the rainwater away, and are ingeniously finished off with pebbles. This is a typical artistic Japanese solution to a practical problem. On the east side of The Old Shoin there is a broad verandah facing the *Gepparo* (Pavilion of the New Moon). Surviving sources ascribe the inspiration for this to the Chinese poet Po Chü-i, who wrote: 'The crescent moon, a pearl fallen into man's heart.' Prince Toshihito was fascinat-

190 *A view of the Shokintei pavilion, Katsura, Kyoto*

◀ 189 *Ama-no-Hashidate, a landscape in miniature, Katsura, Kyoto*

191 *A woodcut by Hishikawa Moronobu:* Garden Pastimes, kemari, *a ball game*

ed by moonlit nights, and had a bamboo terrace built on to The Old Shoin. This was called *Tsukimidai* (a terrace for looking at the moon) and provided a view of the whole garden.

The villa is reflected in the waters of the lake and by taking a boat one can reach pavilions ingeniously situated all over the garden. Facing The Old Shoin, across the water, is the most famous beauty spot of the whole garden, the Bridge of Heaven, a charming replica, built on a scale to suit a garden, of one of the famous beauty spots of Japan.

Beyond the Bridge of Heaven, on the shores of the lake opposite The Old Shoin, lies the Shokintei pavilion (pavilion of pines and the lute). This simple pavilion with its thatched roof is so delightful that it forms the high point of the whole garden. The Shokintei pavilion can be reached from The Old Shoin by a footpath which follows the shore and crosses the lake by a single flagstone. Close to the pavilion, by this flagstone bridge lies the *nagara no chozu* (place where one may wash in the stream). *Tobiishi* lead the visitor to the point where the brook

192 Stone bridge with balustrade. Stone balustrades are rare in Japan

193 Garden path and 'drum' bridge, Onrindo, Katsura, Kyoto

194 *Lake with bridge, Katsura, Kyoto*

runs into the lake and forms a deep pool. Here it serves a similar purpose to that of the water basin by the tea house.

The path then leads the visitor from the *Shokintei* pavilion over a bridge to an island where the *Shokatei* (pavilion of pleasure in blossoms) stands on a low hill. The simplicity of this pavilion is underlined by massive *tobiishi* framed in green moss resting on the slope below. This island also displays one of the later buildings designed for Katsura, *Onrindo,* a little shrine with a pantile roof. A bridge then leads the visitor on to the meadow in front of The New Shoin.

In the south-western part of the garden, by a deep inlet, stands the tea pavilion Shoiken (The House of Smiles), built in rustic style, and standing somewhat apart.

195 *The Gepparo pavilion. The house is open to the garden by means of sliding screens. Katsura, Kyoto*

196 *A scene from the* kabuki *theatre with a backdrop representing a garden scene. Alternatively the action actually takes place in a garden*

197 *View from within a tea house open to the garden, Katsura, Kyoto*

Katsura reveals remarkable artistic values, although at first sight it is perhaps a little too modest. It can only be fully appreciated by those who understand something of Japanese taste expressing the aesthetic values implied in the term *shibui*; this severe simplicity encourages the senses to seek out the beauty in every aspect of nature and human life. In this sense Katsura has wielded a constant influence on Japanese architecture and garden design.

In the middle of the 17th century, about the time when work on Katsura was drawing to a close, work began on another famous Japanese garden, Shugakuin, the Garden of Learning[68]. This garden lies in the north-eastern part of Kyoto, at the foot of Mount Hiei, where, from the 10th century onwards, the emperors turned for some relief from their burden of decision-making. From the records it would appear that the ex-emperor Gomizunoo, at the age of

198 *One of the gates to the lower garden, Shugakuin, Kyoto*

199 *The Chitose covered bridge, Shugakuin, Kyoto*

sixty-one, began the building of Shugakuin in 1655, taking charge of building operations himself.

By its very situation, Shugakuin was bound to enchant all who saw it. Three gardens are arranged on three different levels, giving the whole conception an unusual charm. The path climbs up to the highest terrace, which is the peak of the whole design. One of the gardens was meant for walking in, while the most important features of the lower gardens were the tea houses. The crowning glory of the garden is the *Riuntei* pavilion (the Pavilion that Touches the Clouds). Standing at the highest point of the garden, it offers a magnificent view of

200 *View of the upper garden, Shugakuin, Kyoto*

201 *Tea houses are usually extremely simple. The Riuntei pavilion, Shugakuin, Kyoto*

202 *A composition with three lanterns; the one in the centre is called* sodegata, *the sleeve lamp, and is particularly famous (woodcut)*

the surrounding mountains across the lake. The transition from the garden to the mountains is provided by a belt of trees so skilfully trained that anyone would think they have grown there naturally, without the guiding hand of man.

Shugakuin is famous for the long bands of shrubs trimmed to look like the waves of the sea. The general atmosphere is one of melancholy induced by the gentle curves and the winding paths. The traditional Japanese approach cannot be denied and Shugakuin is typical of the Japanese gardens of the early Edo period, and one of the treasures of Japanese garden art.

203 A landscape of traditional shapes and colours in a contemporary park

The tradition of the *kaiyushiki* garden, represented by Katsura and Shugakuin, has been developed by modern designers in many places throughout Japan today.

204 Traditional garden features in a modern city park, Kokura

205 *An inner garden gate and bamboo fence*

206 *In this garden composition the big boulders associate well with the elegant line of the roof of the old peasant house in the background*

A camellia bloom
fallen
in the shadowy old well.
A sigh.

Buson

House and garden

Throughout the long history of Japanese gardening each of the different styles has produced masterly works of art which count among the treasures of Japanese civilization. They reveal a high degree of skill, taste and feeling for spatial composition and for new and unexpected combinations of forms, colours and structure.

Most valuable of all, however, is the fact that these skills did not remain the privilege of educated aesthetes and craftsmen, fascinated by the idea of transforming art into nature and nature into art, but were taken up by all sectors of society. This is most clearly seen in the type of garden which is most widespread —

207 *A winch was used to move large boulders (woodcut)*

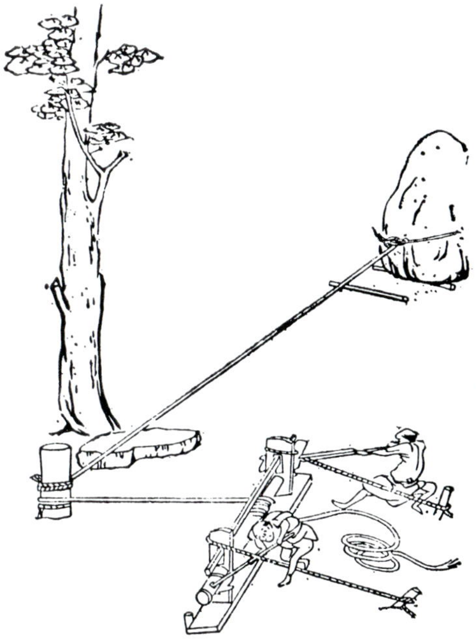

that of the residential garden. Even today, under changing conditions, this remains an integral part of the design of the whole house and contributes to a cultivated way of life.

For the Japanese, their house must be a real home, a place of calm repose where the inmates find at least some relief from the pressures of the social conventions that rule their public behaviour and, in particular, their professional life. There are still many Japanese who return to the traditional way of life the moment the garden gate shuts behind them. They change out of their business clothes into the comfortable yet elegant *yukata*[69], and sit quietly with a bowl of green tea, enjoy a long hot bath or look out at the garden and appreciate the reflection of the sunset or the form of a lateflowering chrysanthemum. Not even the whirl of modern life has so dulled their senses that they cannot delight in the simple things, enjoyed for generations in Japan. The house and the garden provide one of the few places where they can be completely at ease, and where individual pleasures can be fully indulged.

208 *Part of the garden near the gate*

210 *A composition of clipped shrubs against the background of the house*

209 *A design for landscape gardeners showing the division between an inner and an outer garden*

Japan has thus remained a land of beautiful gardens which can be found both in the overcrowded cities and in remote villages. Again and again we admire these masterpieces, and hope that the good taste and imagination they reveal will continue to flourish.

The warm climate enjoyed by most of Japan, and the danger of frequent earthquakes, gave Japanese architecture its characteristic lightness and airiness. Houses are designed to follow a traditional order of proportions which gives plenty of opportunity for individuality, outwardly expressed mainly by the unusual roofscapes.

The interior of the house is no more than an elegant empty space of well-balanced proportions. The yellow *tatami* matting on the floor merges with the brown of beams, pillars and ceilings. The most striking decorative feature is the *tokonoma* recess housing a scroll painting and the *ikebana* flower arrangement, one of the important links between the interior of the home and the garden[70].

A low table with a few cushions on the *tatami* matting around it provide a

symbol for furniture rather than the often cumbersome things themselves in the European sense of the word. All one needs for living is tidied away in wall cupboards or ingeniously planned storage space. Inside the house sliding partitions can be used to form smaller or larger rooms as necessary, and any room can serve equally well as dining room, bedroom or study. One walks on the *tatami* matting in stockinged feet, so that it is relatively easy to keep the rooms spotlessly clean. Such a house has its disadvantages for those members of the family who would like more privacy, but it fits the patriarchal way of traditional Japanese life perfectly.

It is the garden that makes the house a real home. This can be understood from the Japanese word for household, taken from the Chinese, *katei* (*chia-t'ing* in Chinese), formed by the characters for house (family) and garden. The garden is separated from the house by a *shoji,* a sliding screen, of white rice paper.

The Japanese devote a great deal

211 A 'tea-whisk' fence, so named after the shape of the bamboo whisk used in the tea ceremony

212 A design for a small garden, with a water basin, lantern, and 'sleeve' fence (woodcut)

of thought to achieving the closest of bonds between house and garden, not only physically, for here the type of architecture is ideal, but also aesthetically. To be surrounded by a space, however small, which delights the eye and gives a sense of tranquillity, is more important in Japan than any other use to which a garden can be put.

The garden is screened off from its surroundings for complete privacy. In the past, gardens used to be surrounded by a wall, but nowadays fences are preferred. Fences have a long tradition in Japanese gardens and are usually made of wood or bamboo. Their purpose is not so much to keep intruders out of the garden, as to mark it off from its surroundings. Bamboo fences offer the greatest variety, and are often combined with a green hedge or used to provide a backdrop for the flowering trees in the garden. Bamboo fences have different names according to the way they are bound together, the place they come from or the part of the country where they are most popular. The bamboo stems are tied together with simple and complicated knots which are in themselves both functional and beautiful for those with an eye for detail. The most famous knot is the twenty loop knot (Rikyu's knot). These bamboo fences offer a combination of skilled craftsmanship, ingenuity, and the traditional Japanese love for natural materials. Greenery allowed to spring up above the level of the fence or wall relieves the monotony of compact fences and hedges.

The front garden with its gate is usually treated as the place where most contact between the house and outside world takes place, but the traditional Japanese house also has a side gate leading to the kitchen, for servants and tradesmen. As a rule, the front garden is not large, but designed to appear uncluttered.

Some of the old principles of Japanese gardening are usefully employed here. A winding footpath or one with a sharp turn give a greater depth to the scene, especially when irregularly shaped stones are used for the paving. Low bushes by the fence serve the same purpose, and even more effective is a flowering tree planted by the path in such a way that it partially hides the entrance to the house itself.

The Japanese sometimes use a colour contrast between the garden gate and the house entrance; a light-coloured gate and dark front door is considered a good combination. There may be clumps of ornamental grasses by the path, and a stone of

213 *A master fence-maker often designs individual garden gates and fences as well as making them*

214 *Garden gates may be made of bamboo, wicker, laths, matting or planks*

215 *A thickset fence of wicker and bamboo tied with impregnated twine*

216 *Low bamboo fences bound with twine were designed by the painter, potter and landscape gardener Honami Koetsu in the 17th century*

interesting shape by the front door. However, there must always remain enough free space in the garden to prevent any feeling of overcrowding. In earlier times the tap of wooden sandals on the stone path signified that a member of the family was returning home, or that a guest had arrived and must be given a pleasant welcome. Today the front garden is still the place where the first steps into the privacy of a Japanese home are taken.

The living rooms usually face into the garden. An important factor binding house and garden together is the covered verandah. This can be closed with wooden shutters when the weather is bad, providing the house with protection from wind and rain. It also enables the garden to be enjoyed from a slightly elevated position inside the house, since guests are seated on cushions scattered on the *tatami* matting on the floor.

The high standard of landscape gardening in Japan owes much to the fact that designers follow an arts and crafts code that is the result of the experience of generations. Nothing is left to chance, but at the same time there is plenty of room for the expression of individual ideas. The private gardens of Japan are thus an echo of the finest achievements of the past; even the tiniest garden has a link with the perfect compositions of stone or moss found in the famous gardens of Kyoto or elsewhere.

The private garden can be treated as a flat garden (*hiraniwa*), or a garden with artificial hills (*tsukiyama*). The basic elements found in both types are stones, greenery and water in different forms — most usually a little brook, pond or waterfall. The landscape is then completed with bridges, lanterns, a water basin, miniature pagodas and fences, or symbols of these things. Where water is represented purely symbolically in either a flat or a hilly garden, it is called *karesansui* (a dry landscape) as has been described in a previous chapter.

Any type of garden may be treated in one of three styles: *shin* (formal), *gyo* (semi-formal) and *so* (informal). These terms have been taken from the art of calligraphy, where a *shin* style character has exactly the original classical form (*shin* literally means

217 *One of the techniques used in wall building — pantiles bound with mortar*

218 *A garden enclosed by a wall — a common method of delineating space (woodcut)*

219 Garden stream with rocks and clipped bushes along the banks

220 A garden of the so *type with artificial hills (woodcut)*

'true' or 'corrcct'). *Gyo* means 'row' or 'line', and also 'activity'; a *gyo* style character reveals bold brushwork and looks much livelier than the *shin* characters with their rather stiff formality. *So* is a rapidly drawn character; *so* itself is written by the character for 'grass', and the style is often translated as the 'grass style'. It involves fewer strokes and the result is indeed reminiscent of blades of grass moving in the wind. *So* style expresses the calligrapher's individuality, and is greatly appreciated for its original beauty.

Only a calligrapher who has mastered the *shin* style can dare to attempt *gyo* style improvization, while the *so* style calls for the greatest skill of all; the brush moving over the paper freely and without inhibition. These three grades of skill were applied to all the arts and crafts in Japan,

221 *A garden stream. The presence of water, in whatever form, has a powerful effect on the atmosphere and design of a garden*

from the basic mastering of techniques up to the most creative artistic expression.

In the art of the garden *shin* was used for the formal gardens of the most involved composition. *Gyo* represents a freer and more symbolic variant of the formal style. Absolute stylization comes into its own in the *so* style, the garden looking as though it has been designed with a few strokes of the brush.

Instructions for all three styles, as well as illustrated examples, were already part of the medieval gardeners' handbooks[72]. They include a glossary of garden terminology, practical methods, and the creative principles which have become part of the Japanese way of thinking at all levels. Thus a small residential garden can have the same aim as a great landscape garden designed by a famous master: to create in a small space a symbol containing the meaning and essence of nature itself.

All elements of the Japanese private garden must be in harmony with each other, expressed graphically by an irregular triangle called the aesthetic triangle by modern scholars. The three points, *ten-chi-jin*, symbolize heaven, earth and man. For garden design it means linking these three different elements into a single

222 *A cascade is not only a beautiful sight in a garden, but makes a pleasing sound*

223 The garden of a traditional inn (ryokan)

224 Composition: a garden pavilion by a pond

225 *Water pouring from a bamboo pipe. In the evening the water sparkles in the lamplight*

226 *Design for a water basin with a bamboo pipe (woodcut)*

227 *A covered water basin*

whole, horizontally and vertically. It must be applied to each of the individual elements in the garden as well as to the whole composition. Trees and shrubs are planted in accordance with this triangle, as are the positioning of artificial hills, stones, ponds and lanterns.

The elements are arranged in the triangle according to the old principle of *katte*, always from left to right, beginning with the most important of the elements. *Katte* has been a guiding principle in Japanese art, especially in painting and calligraphy, for many centuries.

In order to attain a well-balanced asymmetry it is important to follow the principle of the aesthetic triangle. This is the discipline which gives Japanese gardens their rhythm and feeling of natural growth, although they are, essentially, the most artificial of creations.

The Japanese give the name *yakumono* to those objects which are more important than the others in the garden. It can be applied to a tree, stone, waterfall or a section of a path. It may be a single branch which partially hides the view of the house or the waterfall, but the essential factor is that this is what gives depth to the view.

In this approach, where every

228 A well covered with a roof. Such a feature symbolizes water in the garden even if the well is dry

229 A well with its pulley signifies the presence of water in the garden (woodcut)

single detail is significant, for instance the angle at which a branch is twisted, the way a tree has been clipped, or the exact placing of a stone — there is still plenty of opportunity to ring the changes in the basic design of the landscape. It is for this reason that Japanese gardens do not give a stereotyped impression, and why there is something different to be found in each and every one of them.

The small private gardens provide a good opportunity for the Japanese to display their traditional ability to make the most rational use of the space available; for no space is so small that it cannot be made into a garden.

Fascinating gardens full of surprising ideas are to be found in the narrow entrance to the house, and in the small courtyards behind. The traditional Japanese inns, *ryokan*, which are built in various different shapes and sizes, often have a garden for each of the rooms, creating an intimate atmosphere cut off from the outside world.

Very often a Japanese bathroom will have a broad window looking onto a garden. A hot bath is one of the fundamental pleasures of traditional Japanese life, and to be able to observe the garden while relaxing slowly in a hot bath is a double pleasure.

The traditional garden in front of the living room is not meant for walking in, so much as to be viewed from the verandah or from the room itself. This has influenced its composition. There are numerous devices intended to give the desired depth to a garden

231 *A landscape of mosses and clipped bushes in a flat garden*

◀ 230 *A composition at an entrance to a garden — stone lantern, trees and bushes*

232 *A garden scene with bamboo, pine tree and a flowering plum (woodcut)*

233 *This arrangement of stones against a garden wall makes deliberate use of the 'borrowed scenery' of trees beyond the wall*

of very small proportions. Even the smallest garden looks as though it goes on way beyond the group of conifers which, in reality, mask the fence. The garden path is so laid out that towards the end it bends and twists as though going on into the undergrowth or the depths of the wood, although it may be only a few steps from a busy town street.

Another way of creating an illusion of distance is to plant trees with dense canopies further away from the house, while those with a lighter and more open habit and paler autumn colouring are planted near the house; seen through their delicate branches the garden appears more spacious.

A Japanese garden never lies completely open; the impression aimed

234 House and garden form a unity; the view from inside

235 A flat garden of the shin *type (woodcut)*

236 *A stone lantern, partly shadowed by a pine tree, is placed so as to throw its light on the surface of the lake*

237 *A 'dragon' lantern on a tall pole — partially hidden by a conifer (woodcut)*

for is to open up a new and pleasing vista of beauty and interest every few steps of the way. The neat and tidy garden beds, so familiar in the West, where everything is subordinate to an inexorable symmetry, are completely alien to the Japanese mind. Symmetry excludes the observer from participation in the process of creation, allowing him only a passive role; it kills the imagination instead of encouraging it. In the Japanese view, a mind impoverished and unable to fantasize is incapable of making immediate contact with nature and cannot experience those unique moments of sudden inspiration or profound contentment and inner peace.

The most characteristic example of the Japanese attitude towards the garden is the way they treat stones. It would not be an exaggeration to say that the Japanese are the greatest admirers of stone in the world. They will search for days or even longer in the mountains before finding the one stone they want for a certain spot in their garden. They are particularly appreciative of stones from the beds of mountain streams, or from the seashore. Placed in a garden, such stones become symbols of the scenery from whence they came.

In earlier times ox-drawn carts could be seen on Japanese roads, carrying stones and rocks for great distances. The man in charge of the transport had to see to it that each stone retained its original character. For weeks on end, as he travelled, he would care for a tiny flowering plant that by some miracle had rooted in a crevice of the rock or protect a patch of green moss or grey lichen on the stone from damage.

A wide range of stones, from great boulders to tiny pebbles, are still sold in Japan for garden use. In regions famous for their stones, people will stand by the roadside selling beautiful specimens. It is interesting to note that everybody who has spent some time in Japan instinctively links rushing mountain streams or rocky peaks with the image of a Japanese garden. In part this is due to the careful positioning and choice of stones in gardens.

A carefully chosen stone often gives lifelong pleasure to its owner, who watches it daily and follows all its transformations; whether it is caught by the sun, wet with rain, or lightly powdered with snow — in this way the life of man and the life of the stone are drawn closer together. Japanese gardeners have brought stones to life, displaying their dignity and the patience with which they bear the wind and the beat of the waves.

Stones are used in the garden to make paths, to form a stream bed, to strengthen the shores of lakes and ponds, and alone in symbolic compositions.

As already described in the chapter on dry gardens, the Japanese became highly skilled in the use of stone to form artificial streams, ponds and waterfalls. In these dry landscapes water is only symbolized and stone, gravel and sand are used to create the illusion of the presence of water. This treatment is also found in private gardens, in roof gardens and on the terraces of modern high-rise buildings, where the gardener has only a small space to work within.

Stones are traditionally divided into five or nine kinds, according to their shape and size. It is important not to combine stones of the same size. Stones of natural shape are the most prized, and it is only with great care that gardens can accommodate stones of extraordinary shapes. Gardeners emphasize that there should only be one such stone in any garden, for two or three remarkable stones would destroy the effect. The Japanese have a traditional dislike of stones that are very sharply pointed, considering them difficult elements to fit into a composition. Too many stones are also disapproved of; here, too, moderation and sobriety are always important.

Stones should be placed so as to reveal their face, and to stress their finest qualities, but the Japanese are aware that to make this an unbreakable rule would lead to monotony, and so on occasion the gardener will hide the face of his stone and show the other side.

Boulders are often sunk into the ground to give them the appearance of greater stability and the feeling that they belong to that spot. To give

238 *European and traditional Japanese elements side-by-side in a Nagasaki garden*

239 *Waterlilies on a garden lake*

240 *Garden with artificial hills in the* shin *style (woodcut)*

241 Lake and building in harmony with each other

242 Aquatic plants decorate this lacquer bowl and its lid

a boulder a more massive appearance it is sunk deeper into the ground, giving the impression that it has always stood there. The same effect can also be achieved by planting a tree, not too tall, by the rock to emphasize its size. Shrubs, ferns and grasses are all used to enhance the character of stone. Sometimes, however, stone is used to provide a backcloth for other elements in the garden. Such stones are said to be sacrificed because they have given up their own personality in the interests of overall design.

Besides admiring the shape, the Japanese take great delight in the surface structure and colouring of a stone. They prefer to choose stones grooved in the bed of a stream by the constant rush of water, or worn smooth by the action of the waves on the seashore; but they always select stones which express to them the ideas of age, experience, wisdom, courage, or other good qualities. They are fond of all shades of grey, and especially stones whose surface shows traces of white, pink or blue veining. A fortune would be given for a beautiful stone, for these natural sculptures are the most long-lived part of any garden. Everything else can be washed away by floods, or destroyed by natural disaster such as an earthquake, but stone will persist.

It is also the custom to present a rare stone as a mark of esteem to a best friend.

The Japanese take particular pleasure in the effect of water on stone, and for this reason they can be seen sprinkling a special stone with water, early on a summer's morning or in the evening, to emphasize the freshness of the garden.

Water is an important element in the Japanese residential garden. Little ponds, waterfalls, brooks or even just the small surface of water in a basin symbolize the importance of water in nature and the changes it undergoes during the course of the year. The Japanese make the most of all the different qualities of water. The gentle sound of moving water serves to emphasize the peace and quiet of the garden. They admire its ability to reflect the sky, the green of the trees, the charm of a stone lamp, and above all, the moonlight.

Lakes and streams should look as natural as possible. Lakes are usually irregular in shape, and there are various ways of treating the banks using traditional methods. Stones grouped

243 *The entrance to this modern house uses stones elegantly in an elaborate design*

244 *Flat garden in the* so *style (woodcut)*

245 Suburban garden, Tokyo

246 Modern house and garden, Kyoto

along the banks must look natural and so they are never placed in straight rows. Aquatic plants are grown along the water's edge and bays and inlets are created, with dark pools here and there. Usually a narrow brook runs into a shallow part of the lake and where this happens the pebbles on the bottom should be visible.

A waterfall brings an element of living nature into the garden, even if it is little more than a symbol. It is a basic principle that the waterfall should not be revealed in its entirety, but be admired at one glance. The upper part may be overshadowed by the branches of a conifer, the central part gleams through a shrub and the place where the water falls to the ground may be overgrown with reeds. This creates an optical illusion suggesting that the waterfall is higher and more magnificent than it really is. Both the old and the more modern handbooks for gardeners give illustrations of ten kinds of waterfalls from which to choose.

In small gardens, as in the tea gardens, there is a simple but effective way of making water part of the landscape. It is carried by a bamboo trough or pipe to trickle into a stone basin which in residential gardens is usually purely decorative. These water basins are popular feature as

247 *Ferns are widely used in traditional Japanese gardens*

248 Protecting the trunk of a transplanted tree

249 A Japanese gardener at work training the branches of a tree

250 Training branches along bamboo poles

251 *Flat garden in the* gyo *style (woodcut)*

252 *Trees and shrubs clipped in the* hako zukuri *style*

they enliven the composition of the garden with their long-handled scoops lying alongside.

Choosing a suitable water basin is one of the gardener's delights. They are made in various shapes and sizes and it is a question of personal taste to choose the one which fits in perfectly with the gardener's aim. Sometimes a water basin, a few stones and a fence behind is all that is needed to make a charming corner which would otherwise be wasted.

Another feature of the garden is the stone lantern. Originally this, too, as has already been described in the chapter *A haven of peace,* served a function in the tea garden, throwing a soft light on the path in the evening. Nowadays in residential gardens a lantern is usually a decorative feature. It is best situated to one side of the garden in a shady spot, against a background of trees and shrubs which emphasize its old-world character. Sometimes a tree is planted in front of the lamp, to throw shadows and give it a more interesting appearance.

Almost any plant can be cultivated

253 *A composition of trees, shrubs and stones, against the background of the house*

trees; sometimes working on every single branch to achieve the desired effect. Excessive needle growth is removed from conifers and branches are often trained along lengths of bamboo to create dramatic lines. The trees often look as though they had grown on a windswept cliff, or as if they formed part of a distant mountain landscape.

The changing seasons are sometimes represented in residential gardens by a single tree with blossom

254 *Garden with bamboos*

in a Japanese garden, provided it fits in with the design and atmosphere of the garden and helps to give it a more elegant appearance. It is a notable feature of Japanese life that gardening is an hereditary occupation, families handing down their experience from one generation to the next, mastering new techniques as well as traditional methods, and preserving that rare quality, the touch of the master. They grow trees in such a way that they can be transplanted successfully even when fully grown. However, such trees may need support for years in their new homes and are protected by matting or straw until they have firmly taken root.

Each tree contributes to the final effect of the garden, and both amateur and professional gardeners alike take great care to train their 'key'

255 The azalea festival, Nezu, Tokyo

in spring, green summer foliage, coloured leaves in autumn, dropping to display its winter skeleton of bare branches. Favourite trees displaying seasonal change are the plum and cherry with blossom in spring, the scarlet maple in autumn and in winter the sorbus with its bright orange fruits still clinging to the branches after the leaves have fallen.

Moss, lichens and certain ornamental grasses all help to create the atmosphere of the residential garden. Flowers are not often seen. Those few that are planted are usually different kinds of iris, peonies, lilies and convolvulus; while wisteria, camellia, magnolia and azalea bushes are also popular. *Bonsai* (miniature trees in bowls) are often placed on special ledges in the garden.

Traditional residential gardens can still be found all over Japan, displaying standard elements and compositional forms worked out by many generations of gardeners. Their legacy can still happily be enjoyed by the whole nation as well as providing inspiration to designers and planners from abroad.

Japanese private gardens are striking not only for their beauty, but for their well-balanced composition and the ingenious way they make use of relatively little space. So perhaps for this reason they have become better known abroad than the other styles discussed in this book. There is a growing interest in them today, as modern architecture and urban planning tend to stress the need for unity between the interior of the building and the garden.

256 *Modern hotels are often surrounded by traditional gardens: The New Tagawa Hotel, Kokura*

257 *Gardens can be found on the balconies of apartment blocks*

258 Mount Fuji has always served as a model for artificial hills both in large gardens and in miniature ones

259 Mount Fuji in a miniature garden. Line drawing from an 18th-century book of designs

Miniature gardens and bonsai

The ability to express what is great by what is small, the complicated by the simple and the exceptional by the ordinary, has always been a fundamental principle in Japanese art. That is why the Japanese have so often succeeded in expressing, for example, the spirit of spring in a single twisted branch of plum blossom, or in a few lines of verse like these by Basho[73]:

A peach orchard —
even the oarsmen
stop rowing
for a moment . . .

This approach, very significant for the art of the miniature garden, is as typically Japanese as the seventeen-syllable *haiku* verse form, or an *ikebana* flower arrangement. Like these other art forms, miniature gardens have become the property and the hobby of all classes of people. Today they are particularly popular in the big cities, where a 'garden in a bowl' is often the only contact the city-dweller has with nature.

Whereas in China these miniature gardens have only had one name, *shan-shuei p'en-ting* (a landscape in a bowl), in Japan they have had a succession of names but have now settled for the term *saikei* (live, growing scenery) and this is the name now accepted abroad, particularly in Europe and America. The most frequent names used in the past which the reader may still encounter are *bonsan* (a mountain in a bowl), *bonkei* (scenery in a bowl), *hako-no niwa* (a garden in a box) or *bonseki* (stones in a bowl).

260 *Pine tree whose trunk and branches have been artificially trained. This* bonsai *was seventy years old at the time the photograph was taken*

From the outset the art of creating these tiny gardens was part of the art of the garden as a whole, and it developed into one of the important garden styles. As in the large gardens, each miniature garden had its central motif, and each reproduced a representation of nature or an imagined landscape. The principal difference between the miniature garden and the other styles of gardens was size — in the former case reduced to the miniature proportions laid down by the confines of a pottery bowl. Yet within these limits the gardener managed to express all that can be found in a great landscape garden. It is important to remember that a miniature garden does not offer a deformed likeness, but the mere essence of nature. It gives its creator the chance to deploy his artistic talent and imagination, as well as his skill as a gardener.

261 Bonseki *(a miniature stone garden) from a book of designs*

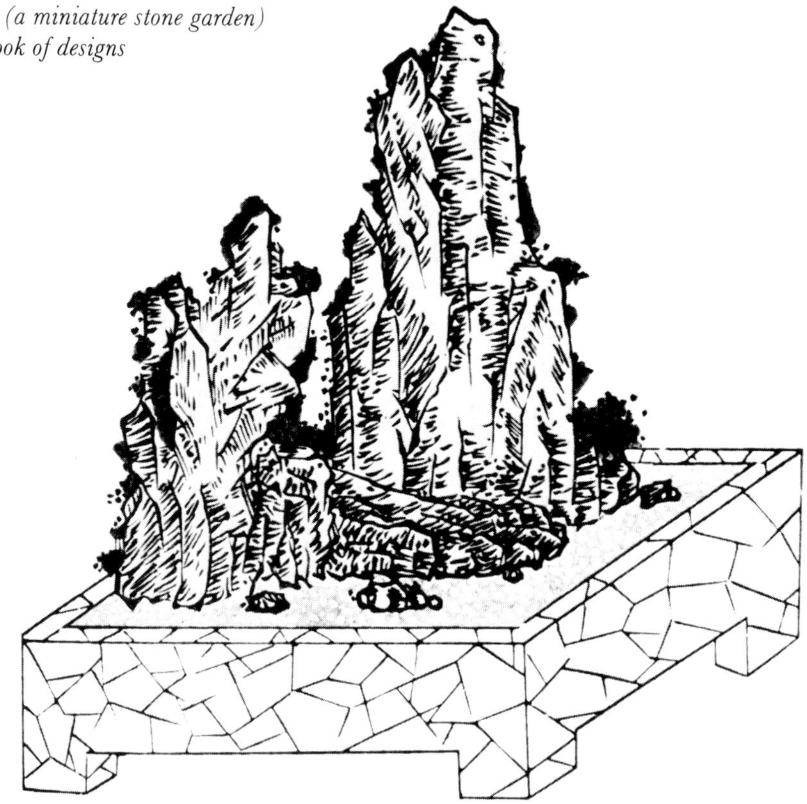

From the earliest historical evidence, the first gardens in a bowl were creations of sand, pebbles, little rocks and greenery arranged to suggest a natural landscape, with perhaps a sacred mountain in the background. Often tiny ceramic figures were added, miniature cottages, bridges and boats. These small gardens became an amusement at court and a popular hobby of the nobility. They seem to have come to Japan from China, between the 6th and 9th centuries, along with other forms of artistic expression and learning. It was probably at this time that

262 *Pine trees growing on a rocky outcrop — a favourite theme for designers of miniature gardens*

gardeners began to grow miniature trees for these gardens in a bowl. Much later these trees acquired the name *bonsai* (grown in a bowl).

From the outset there were close links between styles of garden design and painting. Gardeners often took a Chinese or Japanese landscape painting as their model, or made sketches of natural scenes which caught their fancy. It is interesting to note that some well-known painters took for their subject miniature landscapes which they had created themselves, and become attached to.

264 *Waterfall in a miniature garden. Line drawing from a book of designs*

263 *The island of Natsushima — such an island provided inspiration for designers of miniature gardens*

Together with the other styles of gardening miniature gardens acquired a new philosophical and aesthetic dimension during the 14th to 16th centuries, under the influence of Zen Buddhism. They became an expression of the philosophy of man's relationship with nature.

Paradoxical as it may seem, it was the limited space of the bowl that gave gardeners a new impulse to seek novel ways of attaining their effects by means of symbolism. It was during this period, too, that the principles governing the composition of miniature gardens were drawn up which are still valid today. New styles developed, particularly for dry gardens. Miniature gardens of stones and different kinds of sand were created on lacquer trays. Nevertheless, the mainstream of inspiration was still living plants combined with stones and water, or sand used to represent water.

265 Scene with pine trees painted on a china plate

267 Training the trunks of miniature trees ▶

266 Bonsai *in the* sabamiki *style, with a partially dead trunk. This juniper tree was two hundred and fifty years old at the time it was photographed*

Stones persisted as especially significant elements in the miniature garden, for they can be used to express a broad range of ideas. This is evident from the categories of stones established by collectors. There are stones to represent distant mountains, seashores, cascades, lakes and islands. Most important of all are stones which suggest the thatched roofs of remote cottages which emanate rustic simplicity and calm. Often these stones were — and still are — used alone, to display their natural beauty of form.

Amateur enthusiasts can find the perfect stones for their miniature gardens in the countryside or buy them from specialized nursery gardens. The careful choice of stones and the way they are placed in the bowl can produce in a tiny space the illusion of great distance and the impression of high mountains, a stormy seashore or a calm lake.

However, the features most

admired in these miniature Japanese gardens are the *bonsai*. Growing these tiny trees has become a passion shared by a large proportion of the Japanese people and is one that is accessible to all. The charm of these trees is that although they should not grow taller than 60 to 110 cm (2 to $3\frac{1}{2}$ ft), they possess all the attributes of trees growing in nature. They may reach a great age, in some cases hundreds of years. The oldest *bonsai* in Japan is at least five hundred years old (some think it may even be six hundred); it belonged to the military ruler of Japan, the shogun Iemitsu of the Tokugawa family[7.4]. Today this tree is absolutely priceless. *Bonsai* are family treasures, handed down from

268 A bonsai *nursery*

269 This island of pine trees provides a living model for landscape gardeners

270 Landscape garden in a bowl. Line drawing from a book of designs

271 Miniature gardens ▶

generation to generation. There have been many instances where, in the case of a fire or other catastrophe, the owner of such a treasure has saved it before any of his other possessions.

How is the dwarf stature of *bonsai* achieved? Primarily by cutting back and binding the roots, training the branches in various ways, choosing the correct soil mix and fertilizer balance, regular transplanting and daily care to water and to shade the tree as necessary.

Bonsai growers prefer to work with seedlings from trees which have short

273 *An exhibition of* bonsai *and miniature gardens*

272 *A maple grove in a bowl*

needles or small leaves. The smallest specimens are called 'thimble' *bonsai*, growing to a height of only 3 cm (1 in). 'Bean' *bonsai* are slightly bigger, reaching a maximum height of 6 cm ($2\frac{1}{2}$ in). Most of them originate in rock crevices in the mountains, or come from the drainpipes and pantiles of old temples and houses throughout Japan where they have grown in tiny pockets of accumulated soil.

Bonsai are classified according to shape and sometimes by the number of trunks. The classical style is the formal upright which has a straight trunk like that of a tree in the forest. Another type of *bonsai* is the windswept style with a sloping trunk suggesting a tree growing on cliffs constantly fighting strong winds. Dwarf mountain pines trained in the cascade and semi-cascade styles are a delight, spreading down over the bowl like a green waterfall. A twisted trunk is much admired and assumed to have become contorted during many snowstorms.

At the end of the 19th century, when it became fashionable to

274 A bonsai *of a Chinese quince, seventy years old*

275 A bonsai *juniper tree, 80 cm (2 ft 8 in) high and two hundred years old*

cultivate one's own *bonsai*, growers began to vie with one another to produce trees of bizarre shape, unnaturally twisted. Nowadays the most admired quality is that of natural beauty. Japanese growers object to the use of the term 'dwarf trees' so often heard in other countries.

Trees which have been deformed through the actions of nature, however, are the objects of admiration, and high prices are paid for old trees with a cracked trunk from which new branches have grown. *Bonsai* with several trunks growing from a single root are highly prized, while miniature trees whose roots rise above the soil like waves often carry off the prize in *bonsai* competitions. Trees which bear evidence of a dramatic past are particularly valued, their strange shapes and healed wounds arousing admiration. Growers try to understand the 'feelings' of such a tree, to appreciate the 'experience of life' they represent, so as to incorporate them all the more sensitively in the miniature garden. 'To understand the beauty of a pine means entering into the tree itself and merging with its feelings,' said the poet Basho.

A miniature landscape in a bowl should never be a purely aesthetic rendering of nature; it should express the dynamic changes of nature through the seasons. The slightest tinge of green appearing in the garden bowl in the depths of winter can suggest the delights of spring to come. This is why a gift of a flowering plum, pear or pomegranate *bonsai* or dwarf azaleas is so popular at New Year.

There are over a million *bonsai* growers belonging to Japanese organizations, publishing their own journals and arranging annual exhibitions and frequent competitions all over the country. It is often thought that growing these miniature trees and creating a garden in a bowl are expensive hobbies that only the rich can enjoy. In fact this is an art which is accessible to all. The beginner can buy ready-trained *bonsai* seedlings fairly cheaply in specialist nurseries, where suitable stones can also be bought. Expert gardeners will also advise them on the right kind of bowl or dish to choose. The choice of a bowl is in itself an important aspect of the art, for it gives the miniature garden of the *bonsai* the right framework.

There is also a practical side to the art of the miniature garden, in the small space of the Japanese home. It creates an illusion of nature in conditions in which few have the art to succeed in this way. *Bonsai* and miniature gardens are easily transportable and can be placed wherever they are needed: by the entrance, on a terrace or balcony, or placed for a short while in the *tokonoma,* the alcove in the living room. Wherever it stands, the *bonsai* is always the source of great pleasure.

The principles of miniature gardening and of *bonsai* encapsulate the art of Japanese gardening. They are an art open to everyone, imbued as they are with a beauty and simplicity which can so easily be overlooked or forgotten in the rush of daily life.

276 *Annual exhibitions are held to display flowering* bonsai. *From the azalea exhibition in Isa*

278 Mountain scenery serves as a model for miniature gardens

277 The slopes of a volcano also serve as an inspiration for a bonseki *or* bonkei *bowl*

280 The title page from an 18th-century gardeners' handbook ▸

279 A dry landscape in a bowl from the Hosokawa school, 1969. The sand and stones are from the River Sedo

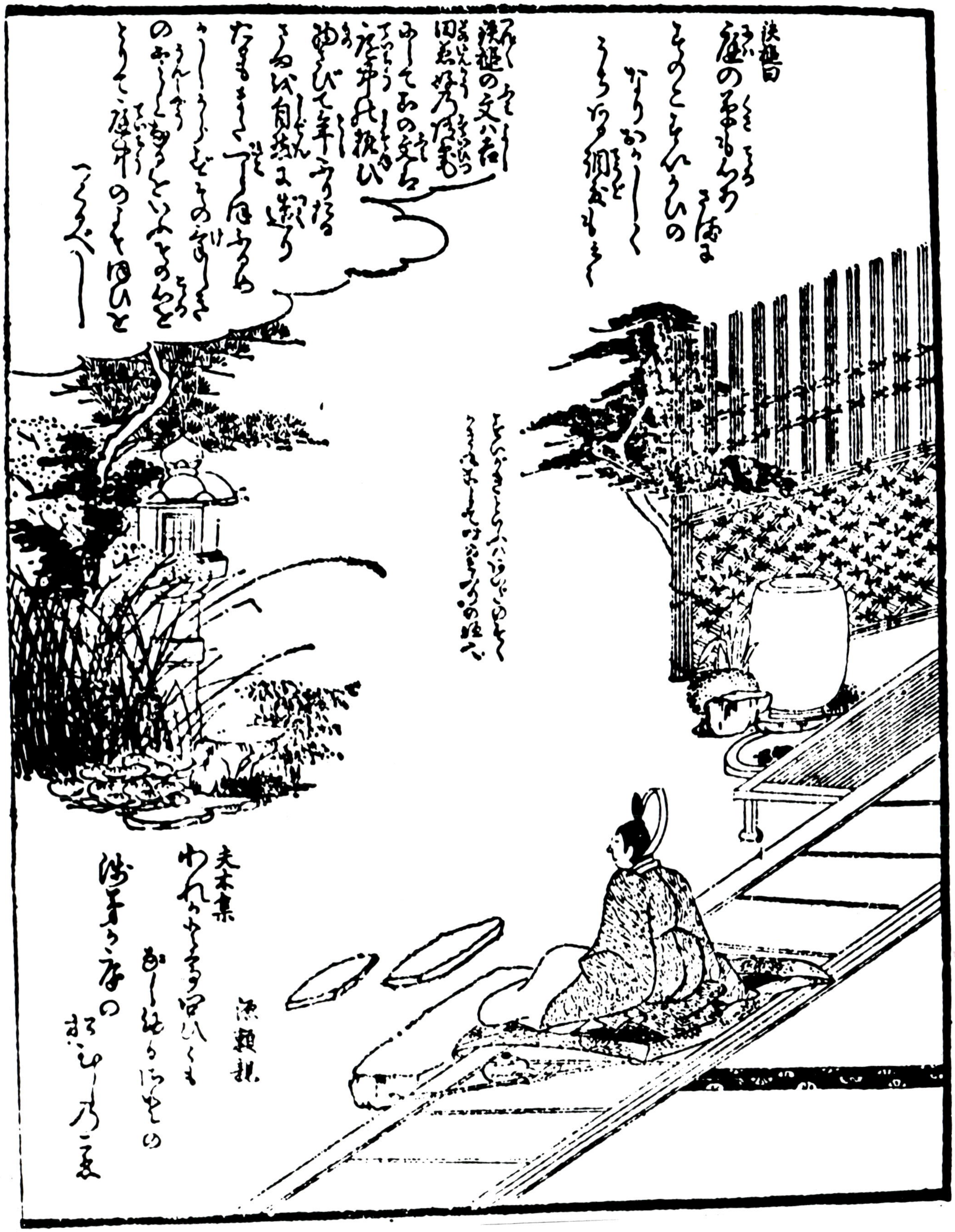

Notes

281 *A flowering shrub in front of the Kotohira shrine, Shikoku*

1) Soami (died 1525), a Zen monk, painter, designer of gardens and authority on their art. The authorship of the book *Tsukiyama sansuiden (Handbook of Landscape Gardening)* is attributed to him.

2) *Haiku,* a Japanese verse form dating from the 16th century, when it expressed the attitudes of the middle classes. The *haiku* always has seventeen syllables, arranged in three lines of five, seven and five syllables respectively. It aims primarily at evoking an atmosphere, and is often inspired by motifs from nature. This form of verse is still being written.

3) T'ang dynasty (618—906 AD). The first reference to Japan in Chinese historical sources dates from the year 57 AD. There are records of contacts between Japan and China in the official Chinese chronicles of the late Han dynasty (25—220 AD) and of the Kingdom of Wei (220—265 AD). They are also mentioned in the historical works Sung-shu (513 AD) and Suei-shu (630 AD), and particularly in the Sin T'ang-shu, compiled in the 11th century AD. According to Japanese historians, gardens of the Chinese type with artificial lakes and hills, with trees and shrubs, were already being laid out in the reign of the Empress Suiko (592—628 AD).

4) Nara period (646—794 AD).

5) Heijokyo, later Nara.

6) Heian period (794—1185 AD).

7) The Japanese began to build barrow tombs for their rulers between the 3rd and 4th centuries AD. Originally placed on natural hill tops, they were later built on artificial hills. They were made up of a circular part and a smaller and lower square part. From the 5th century the tombs were built on the plains. The design and treatment of the barrows are a testament to the highly skilled methods of the gardeners.

8) *Manyoshu,* an anthology of early Japanese poetry in 20 volumes, which dates from the 8th century. It contains 4,500 poems, mostly inspired by nature and the seasons.

9) The *Sakuteiki,* a classic literary work on the art of gardening in Japan. It is attributed to various hands including Yoshitsune Gokyogoku but, in fact, the name of the author is unknown. The book has been designated a national treasure.

The *Sakuteiki* describes gardens laid out in connection with *shinden* architecture in the Heian period. It does not mention the gardens of houses built in the *shoin* style from the 13th century onwards. The book gives instruction in how to lay out a garden, together with systematic descriptions of the materials used and their symbolical significance. The *Sakuteiki* quotes the authority of the landscape gardener Tachibana no Toshitsuna, who lived in the middle of the 11th century, and gives detailed descriptions of gardens laid out during his lifetime. The advice given is accurate and practical; the author says, for instance, '. . . never put big stones anywhere but on the top of a hill or by a waterfall. Do not put stones too close to the house, that they may not stand higher than the level of the floor. Do not lay stones flat that were standing upright in their natural setting, and vice versa.' The author of the *Sakuteiki* attributed religious and even political significance to certain stones. The earth represented the emperor, stones represented the nobles, and water the people. The earth, helped by the stones, directed the flow of the water, and when the earth was no longer firm the water ran where it liked. The lesson to learn was that the emperor should look after his nobles in order to be sure of their support.

The author of the *Sakuteiki* worked out the methods to be used in landscaping gardens with artificial mountains and in flat gardens which were meant to suggest the plains, usually by the seashore or on the banks of a lake.

10) Po Chü-i (772—846 AD) was one of the three greatest Chinese poets. He loved gardens, and in his work showed the importance of a garden for man's inner life. He had a lasting influence on Japanese painters, poets and gardeners. In the 16th century his ideas were interpreted by the painter and landscape gardener, Soami.

11) The Chinese influence is very clear from the earliest descriptions of Japanese gardens. It is known that the courtier Soga no Umako, who died in 626, had a lake made, with an island in it, in the garden in front of his house. The Japanese historian Hirotaro Oka considers it probable that the first gardeners to introduce Chinese ideas into Japan were Korean. They were already laying out landscape gardens complete with artificial hills, lakes and islands.

In the *Elegy on the death of Prince Kusakabe,* in the *Manyoshu,* there is a description of the garden of this late 7th-century prince. It had a lake with rocks on the banks which created the impression of a rocky seashore. Azaleas grew among the scattered stones. The prince's residence was called 'the Place of the Mandarin Orange Island'. It is believed that the gardens of other nobles were similar in style to that of the prince.

12) Emperor Shomu (724—749 AD, or according to other sources, 701—756 AD).

13) *Shoku Nihongi* is one of the earliest Japanese chronicles, and dates from the 8th century.

14) Tosanjoden. The plan of the palace and the garden was reconstructed by Dr Osamu Mori in *Japanese Architecture and Gardens,* Tokyo, 1966, p. 50.

15) Ama-no-hashidate lies in the Bay of Miyazu, north-west of Fuchu, on the island of Honshu. It is a sandy spur not quite 3 kilometres ($1\frac{1}{2}$ miles) long where pine trees grow, twisted by the winds into fantastic shapes. The spur forms the Asoumi lagoon. This beauty spot has often been the subject of paintings and the inspiration for landscape gardens.

16) Emperor Saga (786—842 AD).

17) Lady Murasaki Shikibu (975—1031), the author of *The Tale of Genji,* one of the world's great love stories.

18) Motoori Norinaga (1730—1801), a literary critic whose main subject of study was *The Tale of Genji.*

19) The teachings of the Zen sect of Buddhists came to Japan from China, where it was known as *ch'an*; *zen* means to meditate. In Japan the founding of the sect is attributed to Eisai (1141—1215) and Dogen (1200—1253).

20) Confucianism, which became the state doctrine of

China in the 2nd century AD, brought about many changes in Japan in the 7th century. The prince regent, Shotoku (573—621, or 574—622), applied Confucianist principles to all spheres of life, and in particular used them to concentrate power exlusively in the hands of the imperial court.

21) The Kamakura period (1185—1392). Large expensive gardens were still built during this period, as well as the small gardens around samurai houses in the *shoin* style. The shogun Minamoto Yoritomo, who established the shogunate, was a lover of gardens and considered himself a good landscape gardener. He helped in planning and laying out the Eifukuji garden in Kamakura. The monk Seigen, who was in charge of work on this garden, found rocks of over three metres (ten feet) in height, which he used to create an imposing composition in stone. The garden was completed in 1193. According to the chronicle Azuma Kagami the garden was so lovely that only the nine Buddhist heavens could surpass it. Great landscape gardens around the palaces were also being built in Kyoto at this time, and often there were several hundred men at work on them. Fully grown trees were transplanted, moved carefully in their protective wrappings. The boulders were brought on carts, on special hurdles or by boat. The monk Sadaie, laying out the Saioji landscape garden of Kitayama in Kyoto, had seventeen oxen to draw a famous stone shaped like a lion's head. He also planted mature trees and we learn from contemporary sources that the garden was enchanting: '. . . there were artificial hills there of graceful shape, and a deep forest. The lake was intended to suggest the sea. The waterfall rushed down from such a height that the ground trembled, and the significance of the garden was so profound that it drew tears from those looking at it.'

22) The shoguns of the Ashikaga family were in power from 1338 until 1573.

23) In 1392 the Ashikaga shoguns moved from Kamakura to Kyoto, and the following period of their rule was called the Muromachi period, named after the part of Kyoto where they took up residence.

24) *Sagaryu jiten niwa koho hidensho (The Secret Gardeners' Book of the Saga School)* which, according to Professor Jiro Harada, was first written down in 1395 by a monk named Yasuhira, about whom nothing else is known. The handbook was widely known and later handbooks for gardeners written in the Middle Ages often drew from it. The handbook stressed the need to lay out a garden according to a previously drawn up plan.

25) *Musoryu jiten (Notes on the Muso School).* Abbot Muso is also known under the name Soseki.

26) The dynasty of the Northern Sung (960—1126). The Southern Sung dynasty ruled until 1279.

27) The shogun Ashikaga Takauji (1305—1358).

28) Shubun Tensho (1414—1465) was a painter, a disciple of Josetsu. He studied Chinese and Korean landscape painting and painted in ink in the *shijiku* style, which means literally 'scroll poem'; this was a landscape accompanied by verses or a calligraphic inscription which completed the sense of the painting. Shubun's work expressed the bond between man and nature, and was not without its effect on landscape gardening.

29) The painter Sesshu (1420—1506) was a Zen monk. He spent several years studying in China, where he became acquainted with the Chinese art of the garden. One of his masterpieces is Ama no hashidate, a beauty-spot which not only inspired painters but also landscape gardeners as early as the Heian period. In Sesshu's hands black-and-white landscapes in the Sung style became a true Japanese art. 'Sesshu's line', as it is called, is often described as the supreme artist's line, and his black as perfect black. Contrasting contours of cliffs and rocks are a characteristic feature of Sesshu's landscapes, giving a spontaneous and yet sober evocation of the essential character of a landscape — which is what the landscape gardeners were also trying to achieve.

30) Kokushi means literally 'teacher of the nation', a title which the emperor granted to persons named by the shogun. It was granted to Muso seven times in all, three times during his lifetime and four times after his death.

31) Ashikaga Tadayoshi was the brother of the shogun Takauji.

32) The temple and garden of Saihoji lie on the bank of the River Oi in western Kyoto.

33) The Azuchi-Momoyama period (1573—1615).

34) Ashikaga Yoshimitsu (1358—1408).

35) Ashikaga Yoshimasa (1435—1490).

36) Tenryuji. The original temple buildings were burned down more than once, and those now standing date from the early 20th century. The principal part of the temple was called Tahoden. It is recorded in the temple chronicle that when Muso was restoring the lake he found a stone on which the characters *sogen itteki* were carved, meaning that 'at the beginning every stream is but a single drop'. He therefore gave the name Sogen to the lake, thus creating one of the symbols inspiring Zen meditation on the theme of 'the one in all', for the single drop in whatever form — in a river, cloud, or ocean — is always an indivisible part of nature in its infinite unity. Elsewhere the chronicle refers to the techniques used by Muso in laying out the garden, and the atmosphere he achieved. It records that some trees were planted so as to suggest the whisper of the waves as their leaves rustled, and also that the spirit of Heian times lived on in these gardens.

37) The Emperor Go-Daigo was removed from the throne in 1336 by Ashikaga Takauji, who installed another monarch in his palace, and later himself became shogun. Go-Daigo fled from Kyoto to Yoshino, where he formed his Southern Court. Thus there were two ruling dynasties in Japan up to the year 1392.

38) The shogunate of the Tokugawa family (1615—1868). The period of Tokugawa rule is known as the Edo period.

39) The Meiji period (1868—1912).

40) *Tsukiyama teizoden,* 1735 edition.

41) Ryoanji temple, founded in 1473 by Hosokawa Katsumoto.

42) The Daisen temple was built in 1509 by Rokkaku Masayori. The first abbot was Kogaku Sotan, to whom the building of the famous stone garden and the abbot's house is now attributed. Earlier they were thought to be the work of Soami.

43) Daitokuji temple lies in Murasakino in the northern part of Kyoto and belongs to the Rinzai sect. It was founded in 1324 and has several smaller subordinate temples.

44) Nanzenji temple is a Rinzai temple to the east of the Heian shrine in Kyoto. It was founded in 1293.

45) Kobori Enshu (1579—1647) was a disciple of Furuta Oribe, aesthete, master of the tea ceremony, landscape gardener, painter, poet and art connoisseur.

46) Shodenji temple and garden. The temple was moved to Kyoto from Ichijo Imadegawa in 1282. In the garden, which lies on the east side of the abbot's house, bushes clipped to resemble stones are arranged in groups of seven, five and three. The composition is called Shishi no ko watashi — 'lion cubs swimming across the river' — similarly the groups of stones in the Ryoanji garden are sometimes called 'a family of tigers swimming against the stream'.

47) Myoshinji is the largest monastery of the Rinzai sect in Kyoto and was founded between 1336 and 1338.

48) *Chanoyu* is the name for the tea ceremony which is most common at the present time. It means literally 'hot water for tea', and expresses the elegant simplicity which is the keynote of the ceremony today. The earliest record of tea drinking dates from the reign of the emperor Shomu (724—749), who invited a hundred monks to drink tea with him in the year 728; the tea was brought from China, and the monks listened to him reading sutras. There was certainly a formal ceremony for drinking tea by this time. Some historians maintain that the seed from which tea was first grown in Japan was brought from China in the year 805 by the monk Saicho, also known by his religious name of Dengyo Daishi, the founder of the Tendai sect. A tea plantation exists in Sakamoto, not far from the town of Otsu, where a bush grown from this original seed is still tended. By 815 there was a Tea Office at the imperial court. Other Buddhist monks are also credited with the honour of having introduced seeds of the tea plant. The monk Eisai Zenshi (1141—1215) made the greatest contribution to the ceremonial drinking of tea, for as well as bringing select teas from China, he brought an essay on the tea ceremony and the utensils required for its performance.

49) Sen no Rikyu (1521—1591). Rikyu developed his conception of the tea ceremony in the second half of the 16th century. He first became master of the tea ceremony at the court of Oda Nobunaga (who died in 1582). He later served Toyotomi Hideyoshi, whom he won over to the simple dignity of his conception of the tea ceremony, profoundly influencing its further development and that of the architecture of the tea house and the character of the tea garden. (See also Note 54)

50) Murata Shuko (1422—1509) was master of the tea ceremony at the court of the shogun Ashikaga Yoshimasa, a great patron of the arts. Murata Shuko simplified the ceremony and had it per-

formed in a smaller space. He also introduced scroll paintings and calligraphic inscriptions on the theme of man's relation to nature. He stressed the idea that the tea ceremony should be performed with harmony, dignity, purity and calm.

51) *Wabi* is a very important concept in the Japanese aesthetic code, still valid today.

52) *Sukiya* was the name given to the first tea houses and *sukiya zukuri* is still used to designate the branch of architecture concerned with the tea house. The term is derived from the verb *suki* (to like) and *sukiya* thus means 'a little house where one can drink tea according to one's liking'.

53) *Soan* literally means 'hermitage', and at the same time is used to describe the very simple type of tea ceremony introduced by Murata Shuko. Sen no Rikyu then simplified still further the architecture of the tea house, the style of the garden and the ceremony itself in accordance with the principle of *wabi.*

54) Hideyoshi Toyotomi (1536–1598) was a military ruler of Japan and devotee of the tea ceremony. He was also a patron of crafts, and was responsible for a number of great gardens surrounding luxuriously furnished castles and villas. These were adorned with murals in gold and glowing colours, depicting fantastic subjects. The painters Eitoku (1543) and Sanraku (1557–1635) executed many such murals. Both Hideyoshi and his predecessor Oda Nobunaga filled their gardens with quantities of rare plants, including palms, and hundreds of stones of bizarre shape. Nobles and heads of temples often 'donated' particularly beautiful stones from their own gardens on his express command. Nevertheless Hideyoshi later succumbed to the influence of his master of the tea ceremony, Sen no Rikyu, and realized the significance of a more spiritual beauty and subdued elegance. He had his 'golden' tea chamber knocked down and afterwards drank tea only in a simple tea house of the *soan* type.

55) Furuta Oribe (1543–1615), master of the tea ceremony.

56) *Daimyo* was the name for an important feudal baron.

57) Honami Koetsu (1558–1637) was a painter, potter and landscape gardener.

58) For a list of the principal gardens see: Matsunosuke Tatsui, *Japanese Gardens,* pp. 86–95.

59) Sento gosho, the palace for the retired emperor in Kyoto. Oda Nobunaga had it built in 1571. In the 17th century Kobori Enshu and his brother Kobori Masaharu laid out the garden. It is divided into a northern and a southern part, each with its own lake, and has a five metre (sixteen foot) waterfall. The stones on the banks of the lakes represent a rocky shore. Although the garden has been altered several times, the refined taste of Kobori Enshu can still be felt. The building to which the garden belonged no longer exists.

60) Ogata Korin (1658–1716), painter.

61) Ritsurin, a garden in Takamatsu on the island of Shikoku, is one of the largest and loveliest gardens of the *kaiyu* type. It covers an area of 750,000 square metres (897,000 square yards) and has six lakes and thirteen hills. An older garden laid out on the site as early as 1587 was incorporated in the design. There are three islands in the Southern Lake: Kaedejima (Maple Island), Tokejima (Cuckoo Island), and Tenyojima (Angel Island). The latter is the most interesting from the point of view of garden design; the *hako zukuri* technique was used here, the bushes being clipped to geometrical shapes, squares and cubes. This was a popular technique during the Edo period, but is rarely used today.

62) Gomizunoo (1596–1680) voluntarily abdicated the imperial throne in order to devote himself to calligraphy, poetry and gardening.

63) The Nijo palace in Kyoto was built in the 17th century by the shogun Tokugawa Ieyasu (1601–1603). At first there were no trees in the garden because the falling leaves were too forceful a reminder of the ephemeral nature of all things. There were originally two palaces, but only one has survived. The garden was laid out in 1624 and is attributed to Kobori Enshu, but it has been altered several times since. The most striking feature of the garden are the stone compositions round the lake which has three islands. There is a waterfall in the northeast part of the garden which is also known as Ninomaru.

64) The most important part of Nikko is the mausoleum of the shogun Tokugawa Ieyasu and other members of the family. The layout of the garden round the Toshogu shrine shows the Japanese feeling for uniting the garden with nature. A cedar wood surrounds the buildings, and since the paths were laid later, they wind among the trees very naturally. Garden and architecture form a harmonious whole and the architect Sutemi Horiguchi has described this complex of gardens as 'the perfect landscape garden'.

65) Miyajima, also known as Itsukushima (literally the Temple Island), has a Shinto shrine and lies close to Hiroshima. The shrine rests partially on pillars rising from the sea. It was first built in 811 AD, and has been rebuilt several times. The beauty of the park round the shrine is enhanced by ingenious use of the incoming and outgoing tides; as the tide is coming in, the shrine seems to be floating on the sea.

66) Katsura villa is often described by the Japanese name of Katsurarikyu, the Imperial Summer Palace.

67) Hachijo Toshihito (1579–1629).

68) It was originally planned to start laying out the garden in 1629, but in fact it was not begun until much later.

69) *Yukata,* a summer kimono of cotton.

70) *Ikebana,* a style of flower arrangement, is a widely practised art. Ever since the Middle Ages it was an indispensable part of all social and family occasions, and also of those festivities taking place in house and garden during the year. As we learn from the 'secret' handbooks on flower arrangement, it was especially important to choose the most suitable blossoms or branches, for the *ikebana* were not chosen for their beauty alone, but according to their symbolic significance. They helped to create harmony between the garden and the atmosphere inside the house.

71) Kiyoyuki Nishikara, *Japanese Houses,* Tokyo 1968, p. 133.

72) *Tsukiyama Teizoden,* Tokyo, Kajima shoten, 1975.

73) Matsuo Basho (1644–1694), poet.

74) Tokugawa Iemitsu (1622–1651).

Acknowledgements

The woodcuts are reproduced from mediaeval 'secret' books, mainly from 18th- and 19th-century editions; see Bibliography.

282 *Detail of the roof over the entrance gate at Horyuji*

Bibliography

Bonsan hyakkei zu (*Models for miniature gardens*), 1785.

Chamberlain, B. H.: *Japanese Poetry,* London, 1911.

Coe, Stella: *Ikebana — A Practical Guide to Japanese Flower Arranging,* London, 1986.

Engel, D. E.: *Japanese Gardens for Today,* Tuttle, Tokyo.

Engel, Heinrich: *The Japanese House,* Tokyo, 1964.

Eliovson, Sima: *Gardening the Japanese Way,* London, 1971.

Fujikawa, Asako: *Cha-no-yu and Hideoshi,* Tokyo, 1957.

Fujiwara, Giichi: *Shoin-zukuri kenkyu,* Kyoto, 1976.

Fukukita, Yasunosuke: *The Tea Cult of Japan,* Tokyo, 1955.

Furukawa, Ju: *Karesansui no niwa, Nihon no bijutsu,* no. 61, Tokyo, 1971.

Grigoreva, T. P.: *Yaponskaya khudozhestvennaya traditsiya,* Moscow, 1979.

Hammitzsche, Horst: *Zen in the Art of the Tea Ceremony,* Element Books, 1979.

Harada, Jiro: *A Glimpse of Japanese Ideals,* Tokyo, 1937.

Harada, Jiro: *Japanese Gardens,* Boston, 1956.

Hasegawa, Nyozekan: *The Japanese Character,* Tokyo, 1966.

Hisamatsu, Shinichi: *Zen and the Fine Arts,*Kodansha International, 1982.

Ishizawa, Masao (ed.): *Architecture and Gardens,* Tokyo, 1957.

Kakuzo, Okakura: *The Book of Tea,* Tuttle, Tokyo.

Katsura rikyu to Shugakuin, Iwanami shashin bunko, no. 50, Tokyo s. d.

Kitamura, Iekyusai: *Tsukiyama teizoden,* 1735.

Kitao, Harumichi: *Chashitsu kenchiku,* Tokyo, 1941.

Mori, Un: *Shugakuin rikyu, Nihon no bijutsu,* no. 72, Tokyo, 1972.

Mori, Un: *Shugakuin rikyu, Nihon no bijutsu,* no. 112, Tokyo, 1975.

Nikolaeva, N. S.: *Yaponskie sady,* Moscow, 1975.

Ota, Hirotaro (ed.): *Japanese Architecture and Gardens,* Tokyo, 1966.

Ota, Hirotaro: *Nihon kenchikushi josetsu,* Tokyo, 1962.

Nishikara, Kiyoyuji: *Japanese Houses,* Tokyo, 1967.

Procházka, J.: *O květinách a zahradnictví v Japonsku* (*Flowers and gardening in Japan*), Chrudim, 1930.

Rambach, Pierre: *'L'enigme du Daisen-in', La connaissance de l'art,* no. 127, Paris, 1962.

Sagara, Tokuzo: *Japanese Fine Arts,* Tokyo, 1958.

Sansom, G. B.: *A Short Cultural History,* Ruthland and Tokyo, 1952.

Scheidl, Leopold: *Die geographischen Grundlagen des Japanischen Wesens,* Tokyo, 1937.

Senkeiban zushiki (*Models for miniature gardens*), 1826.

Shigemori, Kanto: *The Japanese Country and Garden,* Weatherhill, Tankosha.

Shoten, Kajima (ed.): *Tsukiyama teizoden, 1734,* Tokyo, 1965.

Suisho Nihon no meien: *Kyoto Rinsen Kyokay,* Kyoto, 1978.

Suzuki, Daisetzu: *Zen and the Japanese Culture,* Routledge & Kegan Paul.

Suzuki, D. T.: *Zen Buddhism,* New York, 1956.

Swinton, Anne: *The Collingridge Handbook of Bonsai,* Twickenham, England, 1986.

Takugawa, Gisei: *Meien no saguru,* Kyoto, 1965.

Tamura, Tsuoshi: *Art of the Landscape Garden in Japan,* Tokyo, 1947.

Tange, Kenzo: *Arkhitektura Yaponii,* Moscow, 1975.

Tatsui, Matsunosuke: *Japanese Gardens,* Tokyo, 1969.

Tsunoda, Ryusako, Barry, Wm. Theodore and Keene, Donald (eds.): *Sources of Japanese Tradition,* New York, 1958.

Ueda, Makoto: *Literary and Art Theories in Japan,* Cleveland, 1967.

Watts, Alan W.: *The Way of Zen,* New York, 1962.

Woollard, Leslie: *Japanese and Miniature Gardens,* Magna.

Yoryo zukuri niwa no zo, Tokyo, 1975.

283 A water basin with scoops at the entrance to a temple garden

Index

Figures in italics indicate plate numbers

284 An arrangement of metal lanterns, Daiyuin, Nikko